KU-626-970

Selection of Florence
Hotels and
Restaurants

Where do you start? Choosing a hotel or restaurant in a place you're not familiar with can be daunting. To help you find your way amid the bewildering variety, we have made a selection from the *Red Guide to Italy 1990* published by Michelin, the recognized authority on gastronomy and accommodation throughout Europe.

Our own Berlitz criteria have been price and location. In the hotel section, for a double room with bath but without breakfast, Higher-priced means above L. 300,000, Medium-priced L. 125,000–300,000, Lower-priced below L. 125,000. As to restaurants, for a meal consisting of a starter, a main course and a dessert, Higher-priced means above L. 45,000, Medium-priced L. 35,000–45,000, Lower-priced below L. 35,000. Special features where applicable, plus regular closing days are also given. As a general rule many Florence restaurants are closed in August. For hotels and restaurants, both a check to make certain that they are open and advance reservations are advisable. In Florence restaurants, 12–15% service charge will be added to the bill.

In Florence, hotel reservations can be made at the I.T.A. counter at the railway station.

For a wider choice of hotels and restaurants, we strongly recommend you obtain the authoritative Michelin *Red Guide to Italy,* which gives a comprehensive and reliable picture of the situation throughout the country.

HOTELS

HIGHER-PRICED
(above L. 300,000)

Excelsior
piazza Ognissanti 3
50123 Florence
Tel. 264201
Tlx. 570022
205 rooms
*Summer restaurant service on
terrace with view.*

Grand Hotel Villa Cora
viale Machiavelli 18, Colli (3 km.)
50125 Florence
Tel. 2298451
Tlx. 570604
48 rooms
*Pleasant hotel. Flower-park with
outdoor swimming pool. Taverna
Machiavelli restaurant.*

Regency
piazza Massimo d'Azeglio 3
50121 Florence
Tel. 245247
Tlx. 571058
38 rooms
Pleasant hotel. Charming garden.

Villa La Massa
Candeli
50010 Florence
Tel. 630051
Tlx. 573555
38 rooms
*18th-century building, furnished in
period style. Quiet hotel. Heated*

*outdoor swimming pool. Garden.
Hotel tennis court. Il Verrocchio
restaurant.*

Villa Medici
via Il Prato 42
50123 Florence
Tel. 261331
Tlx. 570179
107 rooms
*Outdoor swimming pool.
Outdoor dining.*

MEDIUM-PRICED
(L. 125,000–300,000)

Baglioni
piazza Unità Italiana 6
50123 Florence
Tel. 218441
Tlx. 570225
195 rooms
Roof-garden restaurant with view.

Continental
lungarno Acciaiuoli 2
50123 Florence
Tel. 282392
Tlx. 580525
61 rooms
*Flowered terrace with view.
No restaurant.*

Crest
viale Europa 205
50126 Florence
Tel. 686841
Tlx. 570376
92 rooms
*Heated outdoor swimming pool.
Garden. La Tegolaia restaurant.*

Della Signoria
via delle Terme 1
50123 Florence
Tel. 214530
Tlx. 571561
27 rooms
No restaurant.

Grand Hotel Minerva
piazza Santa Maria Novella 16
50123 Florence
Tel. 284555
Tlx. 570414
96 rooms
Outdoor swimming pool.

Jolly
piazza Vittorio Veneto 4/a
50123 Florence
Tel. 2770
Tlx. 570191
167 rooms
Outdoor swimming pool on panoramic terrace.

Kraft
via Solferino 2
50123 Florence
Tel. 284273
Tlx. 571523
68 rooms
Roof-garden restaurant with view. Outdoor swimming pool.

Lungarno
borgo Sant'Jacopo 14
50125 Florence
Tel. 264211
Tlx. 570129
68 rooms
View. Collection of modern paintings. No restaurant.

Montebello Splendid
via Montebello 60
50123 Florence
Tel. 298051
Tlx. 574009
41 rooms
Garden.

Plaza Hotel Lucchesi
lungarno della Zecca Vecchia 38
50122 Florence
Tel. 264141
Tlx. 570302
97 rooms
View.

Principe
lungarno Vespucci 34
50123 Florence
Tel. 284848
Tlx. 571400
21 rooms
View. Garden. No restaurant.

Relais Certosa
via Colle Ramole 2, Galluzzo
(6,5 km.)
50124 Florence
Tel. 2047171
Tlx. 574332
69 rooms
View. Garden. Hotel tennis court.

Villa Belvedere
via Benedetto Castelli 3, Colli
(3 km.)
50124 Florence
Tel. 222501
Tlx. 575648
27 rooms
Quiet hotel. View of city and hills. Outdoor swimming pool. Tennis court. No restaurant.

Villa Carlotta
via Michelle di Lando 3, Colli
(3 km.)
50125 Florence
Tel. 220530
Tlx. 573485
26 rooms
Quiet hotel with charming garden.

Villa le Rondini
via Bolognese Vecchia 224 (7 km.)
Trespiano
50139 Florence
Tel. 400081
Tlx. 575679
33 rooms
*Set amid olive trees. Outdoor
swimming pool. Hotel tennis
court.*

Villa Liberty
viale Michelangiolo 40
50125 Florence
Tel. 6810581
16 rooms
Garden. No restaurant.

Ville sull'Arno
lungarno Colombo 5
50136 Florence
Tel. 670971
Tlx. 573297
47 rooms
*View. Heated outdoor swimming
pool. No restaurant.*

LOWER-PRICED
(below L. 125,000)

Astor
viale Milton 41
50129 Florence
Tel. 483391
Tlx. 573155
23 rooms

Balestri
piazza Mentana 7
50122 Florence
Tel. 214743
50 rooms
No restaurant.

Calzaiuoli
via Calzaiuoli 6
50122 Florence
Tel. 212456
Tlx. 580589
37 rooms
No restaurant.

Caravel
via Alamanni 9
50123 Florence
Tel. 217651
59 rooms
No restaurant.

David
viale Michelangiolo 1
50125 Florence
Tel. 6811696
Tlx. 574553
25 rooms
No restaurant.

Fiorino
via Osteria del Guanto 6
50122 Florence
Tel. 210579
23 rooms
No restaurant.

Golf
viale Fratelli Rosselli 58
50123 Florence
Tel. 293088
Tlx. 571630
39 rooms
No restaurant.

Jane
via Orcagna 56
50121 Florence
Tel. 677383
24 rooms
No restaurant.

Rapallo
via di Santa Caterina
d'Allessandria 7
50129 Florence
Tel. 472412
Tlx. 574251
30 rooms

Royal
via delle Ruote 52
50129 Florence
Tel. 483287
29 rooms
Pleasant garden. No restaurant.

Silla
via dei Renai 5
50125 Florence
Tel. 2342888
32 rooms
No restaurant.

RESTAURANTS

HIGHER-PRICED
(above L. 45,000)

Antico Crespino
largo Enrico Fermi 15, Colli
(3 km.)
50125 Florence
Tel. 221155
View. Closed Wednesday.

Cammillo
borgo Sant'Jacopo 57
50125 Florence
Tel. 212427
*Typical Florentine trattoria.
Closed Wednesday and Thursday.*

Da Noi
via Fiesolana 46
50122 Florence
Tel. 242917
*Notably good cuisine. Reservation
essential. Closed Sunday and
Monday and at lunchtime.*

Enoteca Pinchiorri
via Ghibellina 87
50122 Florence
Tel. 242777
*Excellent cuisine. Evening service
in cool courtyard. Reservation
essential. Closed Sunday, and
Monday lunchtime.*

Harry's Bar
lungarno Vespucci 22
50123 Florence
Tel. 296700
*Reservation essential. Closed
Sunday.*

Lume di Candela
via delle Terme 23
50123 Florence
Tel. 294566
*Reservation essential. Closed
Sunday and Monday lunchtime.*

Sabatini
via de Panzani 9/a
50123 Florence
Tel. 282802
*Elegant traditional decor. Closed
Monday.*

MEDIUM-PRICED
(L. 35,000–45,000)

Al Campidoglio
via del Campidoglio 8
50123 Florence
Tel. 287770
Closed Thursday.

Buca Lapi
via del Trebbio 1
50123 Florence
Tel. 213768
*Typical taverna.
Closed Sunday, and Monday at
lunchtime.*

Buca Mario
piazza Ottaviani 16
50123 Florence
Tel. 214179
*Typical trattoria. Closed
Wednesday, and Thursday at
lunchtime.*

Cafaggi
via Guelfa 35
50129 Florence
Tel. 294989
*Closed Sunday evening and
Monday.*

Cavallino
via delle Farine 6
50122 Florence
Tel. 215818
*Typical habitues' restaurant.
Outdoor dining in summer with
view.*

Celestino
piazza Santa Felicita 4
50125 Florence
Tel. 296574
Closed Sunday.

13 Gobbi
via del Porcellana 9
50123 Florence
Tel. 298769
*Tuscan specialities. Closed
Sunday and Monday.*

Il Profeta
borgo Ognissanti 93
50123 Florence
Tel. 212265
Closed Sunday and Monday.

La Loggia
piazzale Michelangiolo 1
50125 Florence
Tel. 2342832
*Outdoor dining in summer with
view. Closed Wednesday.*

Lo Strettoio
Serpiolle (8 km.)
50142 Florence
Tel. 403044
*17th-century villa amid olive
grove. Outdoor dining. By
reservation only. Closed Sunday
and Monday.*

Paoli
via dei Tavolini 12
50122 Florence
Tel. 216215
*Typical restaurant. Reproduction
14th-century-style decor. Closed
Tuesday.*

Trattoria Vittoria
via della Fonderia 52
50142 Florence
Tel. 225657
*Seafood specialities. Closed
Wednesday.*

LOWER-PRICED
(below L. 35,000)

Il Caminetto
via dello Studio 34
50122 Florence
Tel. 296274
*Outdoor dining. Closed
Wednesday.*

Il Fagioli
corso Tintori 47
50122 Florence
Tel. 244285
*Typical Tuscan trattoria. Closed
Sunday and also on Saturday in
summer*

Il Tirabusciò
via de' Benci 34
50122 Florence
Tel. 2476225
*Reservation essential. Closed
Wednesday and Thursday.*

La Carabaccia
via Palazzuolo 190
50123 Florence
Tel. 214782
*Closed Sunday and Monday
lunchtime.*

Le Quatro Stagioni
via Maggio 61
50125 Florence
Tel. 218906
*Reservation essential. Closed
Sunday.*

Omero
via Pian de' Giullari 11 (5 km.)
Arcetri
50125 Florence
Tel. 220053
*Country trattoria with view.
Summer dining on terrace. Closed
Tuesday.*

Pierot
piazza Taddeo Gaddi 25
50142 Florence
Tel. 702100
Closed Sunday.

BERLITZ®

FLORENCE

By the staff of Berlitz Guides

15th edition (1992/1993)

Updated or revised 1991, 1990, 1987, 1985, 1983,
1982, 1981, 1980

QUI

DOVE A DIFESA DELLA LIBERTÀ

STETTE MICHELANGIOLO

GLI ERESSE CON OPERE DELLA SUA MANO

MONUMENTO DEGNO

LA PATRIA

How to use our guide

- All the practical information, hints and tips that you will need before and during the trip start on page 98.

- For general background, see the sections Florence and the Florentines, p. 6, and A Brief History, p. 10.

- All the sights to see are listed between pages 20 and 72, with suggestions for daytrips from Florence from page 73 to 81. Our own choice of sights most highly recommended is pinpointed by the Berlitz traveller symbol.

- Entertainment, nightlife and all other leisure activities are described between pages 82 and 89, while information on restaurants and cuisine is to be found on pages 90 to 97.

- Finally, there is an index at the back of the book, pp. 126–128.

Although we make every effort to ensure the accuracy of all the information in this book, changes occur incessantly. We cannot therefore take responsibility for facts, prices, addresses and circumstances in general that are constantly subject to alteration. Our guides are updated on a regular basis as we reprint, and we are always grateful to readers who let us know of any errors, changes or serious omissions they come across.

Text: Lyon Benzimra
Photography: Jean Mohr
Layout: Doris Haldemann
We wish to thank Simone Bargellini, Michael H. Sedge, the Italian National Tourist Office and the Azienda Autonoma di Turismo for their assistance with this guide.
Cartography: 🌀 Falk-Verlag, Hamburg.

Contents

Cover picture: Ponte Vecchio
Photo, pp. 2–3: On the Piazzale Michelangelo

5

Florence and the Florentines

You must take Florence for what it is: one of History's phenomena. Few nations, let alone cities, can boast such an overpowering array of talent—literary, artistic, political—concentrated over so short a period of time. The names of some of Florence's greatest sons—Dante, Boccaccio, Giotto, Donatello, Botticelli, Leonardo, Michelangelo, Cellini, Machiavelli—are well known the world over. Not a bad achievement for a city whose great period spanned less than 300 years.

Guidebooks often compare Renaissance Florence with 5th-century Athens, but while only spectacular ruins are left of that ancient Greek splendour, Florence is much more than a museum of stone, marble and bronze. Its historic palaces, its great churches, its innumerable works of art are not dry-as-dust relics. They're very much lived-in, worked-in, prayed-in and prized by today's Florentines.

Walking through this amazing city is likely to give you a pain in the neck—literally. There's so much to look at, simultaneously and at every level: a row of shop-windows, a courtyard glimpsed through a *palazzo* gateway, a faded street shrine lit by flickering oil lamps, a worn coat-of-arms, a commemorative plaque, rusted, centuries' old tethering rings and torch-holders. And, higher still, loom the stony masses of the *palazzi*—from medieval fortress dwellings and Renaissance mansions to heavily ornate 17th-century buildings—with names like Acciaiuoli, Rucellai, Strozzi, Pazzi, Salviati, Medici, straight out of history.

You won't feel that time has stood still here. The centre's bustle, its noisy, smelly (though now restricted) traffic, are very much part of the late 20th century. Yet most of the city's main streets are as narrow and their paving as uneven as they've ever been; the *palazzi*

The Arno, once a vital artery, has kept its picturesque bridges. 7

are little changed and the voices you'll hear, melodious or harsh, with that unique Florentine pronunciation, would still sound familiar to Dante.

Through the centre of the city flows the muddy green Arno, bordered by broad *lungarni,* or embankments, built last century to protect against flooding. Spanning the river is the Ponte Vecchio, one of the oldest and most unusual bridges in the world, known for its goldsmiths' and jewellers' boutiques since the 16th century. Before that it was the domain of the butchers, the Arno being useful for waste disposal.

The craft tradition, a fascinating aspect of Florentine life, is typical of the city's genius for combining art and business. Every district has its artisans—ropemakers, bookbinders, embroiderers, wrought-iron workers or even gold-leaf beaters. In the back streets of the left bank, full of reproduction "factories", the mellow smell of varnish, wax and wood will assail you from many a doorway as you pass.

You may find Florentines disappointingly "un-Italian" in their behaviour. As a whole they're less forthcoming with tourists than, say, Neapolitans or Romans. They're courteous with strangers but refuse to pander to them. You'll experience little of that traditional Italian exuberance, apart maybe from an occasional exchange of street insults in thick Tuscan. But then, the Florentines, like their city, are an exception to the rule.

Hard-working, inventive, sharp-witted: these qualities still describe the natives of Florence. Add to that an inborn sense of dignity and sober elegance, a biting, often cruel wit, a savage pride in their city, a remarkable cockney-like resilience in adversity.

The November 1966 flood disaster (the worst of 50 floods in the city's history) was a supreme example of that resilience. Swollen by heavy rains, the Arno burst its banks one night, carrying all before it. In certain parts of the city, it reached depths of 23 feet. Thick mud, as well as oil from burst central-heating tanks, swirled everywhere. Hundreds of paintings, frescoes, sculptures and over a million priceless old books suffered incalculable damage. The people of Florence rose to the challenge.

Young Florentines still rendezvous on medieval Ponte Vecchio.

Before the flood waters had even receded the city's works of art were being lovingly rescued, and the long, hard job of restoring them immediately begun.

While some restoration continues, most of the damaged works have been repaired and are again displayed in museums and galleries throughout Florence. So now, the city of the arts since the 15th century is ready to welcome you in its full splendour.

A Brief History

No one quite knows how Florentia, Fiorenza or Firenze as it's now called came by its name. According to some, it was named after Florinus, a Roman general who encamped in 63 B.C. on the city's future site and from there besieged

Musicians in full regalia for Scoppio del Carro festivities.

the nearby, powerful Etruscan hill town of Fiesole.

Whatever the origin Roman Florence began to develop seriously around 59 B.C., becoming a thriving military and trading town. When you walk along Via Romana and on over Florence's famed Ponte Vecchio towards the city centre, you'll be treading the same ground Roman legions, travellers and merchants trod. And though you'll find no visible Roman remains in Florence (you'll have to visit Fiesole for that), all the trappings of civilized life were to be found here, from baths and a forum to temples and a theatre.

The barbarian invasions and the fall of the Roman empire plunged Europe into a dark, chaotic period. Lombards succeeded Goths, then came a temporary ray of light with Charlemagne's great 8th–9th-century European empire, but by the next century even greater chaos had set in.

Somehow the Carolingian province of Tuscany survived. In the late 11th century, Florence made rapid commercial and political progress under a remarkable ruler, Countess Matilda. The great guilds *(arti)* —wool and silk merchants, spice merchants, apothecaries, etc.—began to develop, and by 1138, 23 years after Matilda's death, Florence was a self-governing republic and a power to be reckoned with.

At that time the city must have presented a strange picture. All the great families had square stone towers (often more than 230 feet high!) built adjoining their houses—impregnable refuges during those ever-recurring feuds. By the end of the 12th century, the city's skyline bristled with over 150 of them (like San Gimignano today). They've all long since disappeared.

Guelphs and Ghibellines

Florence's history might then have been clear sailing but for the savage factional struggles. Sooner or later the interests of an aristocratic caste and a rising merchant class were bound to clash: the nobility opposed the broader based forms of government the merchants sought. Fierce inter-family feuds and continual raids on Florentine trade by "robber barons" did little to help.

Worst of all, powerful foreign interests became involved. The Guelph and Ghibelline parties, which developed in the 13th century, had ties outside Florence: the Guelphs tended to support the Pope, while the **11**

Ghibellines looked to the Holy Roman Emperor. Further complicating matters was the French monarchy; it took a special interest in Florentine developments—ever ready to interfere in and profit from the fratricidal strife.

Other Tuscan cities followed suit with their own Guelph-Ghibelline parties and, for over two centuries, Tuscany was in a state of turmoil as first the aristocratic Ghibellines then the burgher Guelphs gained power. Defeated leaders were exiled with their families and followers, their property confiscated or destroyed. From friendly cities they plotted their return and the whole sorry cycle would begin once more. Pisa, Lucca, Pistoia, Siena, Arezzo, Florence were enemies at one time, allies at another, depending on which party held power.

Yet despite all this, Florentine commerce and banking continued to develop. Its woollen-cloth trade prospered; the first gold florin was minted there in the mid-13th century, and then rapidly adopted everywhere in Europe as a handy unit of coinage. Florence's social evolution over the 13th and 14th centuries was also remarkable: organized "factories" or workshops were opened; hospitals, schools and charitable societies founded; its university (one of Europe's oldest) turned out lawyers, teachers and doctors by the score; streets were paved, laws were passed regulating noise and nuisance; a kind of early Red Cross (the Brotherhood of the Misericordia, see p. 30) was formed. Life was hard, people toiled, but no one was allowed to starve to death. Never a democracy in the modern sense of the term, Florence nonetheless gave its citizens a unique sense of "belonging" that overrode class or party differences.

In spite of their internal divisions, the Guelphs gradually edged the Ghibellines completely out of power. By the late 13th century, the bankers', merchant and craft guilds reigned supreme in the Florentine republic, secure enough to turn their attention to building a fitting seat of government. With a sumptuous cathedral already under way, a mighty People's Palace (Palazzo del Popolo, later Palazzo della Signoria or Palazzo Vecchio) was begun in 1298. It still serves today as Florence's city hall.

Domenico di Michelino's Dante Explaining His Divine Comedy.

Florentine Men of Letters

DANTE ALIGHIERI (1265–1321), member of a Guelph family, was exiled by a faction of his party for the last 19 years of his life. His immortal poem, *The Divine Comedy*, a journey to Paradise via Hell and Purgatory, is one of the great turning points in world literature. In it he presents a double vision: the political and social order as divinely ordained and the ugly reality of the corrupt society around him.

One of the world's most translated authors, Dante wrote his masterpiece not in the usual scholarly Latin but in everyday language for all to understand. His work established the Tuscan vernacular as Italy's literary language.

Dante is especially remembered because of his unrequited love for Beatrice Portinari—yet he was only nine when he first set eyes on her.

GIOVANNI BOCCACCIO (1313–75) was a classical scholar and university lecturer, specializing on Dante. Surviving the Black Death, he used his experiences as the inspired basis for his marvellous, racy prose tales, *The Decameron*. Written in an Italian which is still easily understood, the work is unrivalled for gentle eroticism, humour and vivid characterization.

Dawn of a Golden Age

Florentine bankers now held the purse-strings of Europe, their agents based in every major city. One group headed by the Bardi and Peruzzi families lent Edward III of England a staggering 1,365,000 gold florins, for his campaigns against the French. But Edward's sudden double-dealing declaration of bankruptcy in 1343 had unexpectedly toppled the entire Florentine banking structure.

Yet the resilient Florentines recovered; the merchant interests set out with ruthless zest to regain their lost prestige. Despite continuing social unrest, violent working-class riots, flood, famine and the Black Death of 1347–48 which killed off about half of Florence's population, the city found itself by the early 1400s stronger and richer than it had ever been.

The power of the important business families, the *signori,* had proved greater than that of the guilds. The way now lay open for the Medici, wealthy wool merchants and bankers, who were to dominate every facet of Florentine life and culture for 60 golden years (1434–94). They led the city and its people to unparalleled heights of civilization, while most of **14** Europe struggled to free itself from the coarse, tangled meshes of medieval feudalism.

Yet even before the Medici ushered in this golden age there were already signs of that great Italian Renaissance which started in Florence. Interest in long-neglected Latin and Greek literature was reviving; Florentine historians were busy recording their city's progress for posterity; merchant guilds and nouveaux-riches with money to burn or consciences to appease found time between business deals and party vendettas to indulge in artistic patronage.

In spite of their factions, the Florentines envisaged ambitious public works and imposing private *palazzi:* the Duomo, Giotto's Campanile, the great monastic churches of Santa Croce and Santa Maria Novella, the Bargello, the Palazzo della Signoria were begun or completed in that tumultuous 14th century.

The Renaissance

The term "Renaissance" was coined by a 16th-century Florentine artist, Giorgio Vasari whose *Lives of the Painters* still makes fascinating reading and tells us virtually everything we know about the great Italian artists from the 13th century to his own time.

Renaissance means rebirth

and that's exactly what it was: men appeared to be waking from a long sleep and taking up life where antiquity had left off.

Throughout the Middle Ages the Church had dominated the cultural life of Europe. Literature, architecture, painting, sculpture, music were all geared to glorifying God rather than earthly life and beauty. The Greek and Roman ideal of "art for art's sake" had been forgotten. The Florentines revived this concept. When you visit the Uffizi, compare Cimabue's *Virgin Enthroned* with Botticelli's *Primavera,* painted 200 years later. The two works epitomize the difference between the Middle Ages and the Renaissance.

In those uncertain times the idea took hold that life must be lived to its fullest, that pursuit of earthly knowledge, beauty and pleasure were what really counted in the brief span of life alloted to man. The arts and sciences of the Renaissance were directed to that end.

A 19th-century German scholar wrote it off as "an intellectual bacchanalia"; but Lorenzo de' Medici—*il Magnifico* as his contemporaries dubbed him for his patronage of art and scholarship—summed it up with greater charm:

SCALA, Florence

Lorenzo il Magnifico: merchant, politician, patron of the arts.

Quant'è bella giovinezza,
che si fugge tuttavia!
Chi vuol esser lieto sia:
di doman non c'è certezza.

How fine a thing is youth
   but how short-lived.
Let he who wishes to be merry,
   be so.
For there's no saying what
   tomorrow will bring.

15

The author of these sentiments had seen his 25-year-old brother Giuliano savagely murdered at his side during mass in the Duomo by members of the rival Pazzi family (1478).

The Medici Hold

Remarkably enough, few of the early Medici ever held office in the city government. Yet Cosimo the Elder (1389–1464), a munificent patron of the arts and letters, who earned himself the title *pater patriae* (father of his country), his son Piero "the Gouty" (1416–69) and his grandson Lorenzo the Magnificent (1449–92) were rulers of Florence in all but name. Ably pulling the strings through supporters elected to the republican Signoria, or government, all three were expert politicians who knew how to woo the Florentine masses.

Poet, naturalist, discerning art collector, would-be architect, a dabbler in philosophy, in other words a typical Renaissance generalist, Lorenzo was perhaps the most outstanding member of the Medici family. His diplomatic skill kept Italy temporarily free of wars and foreign invasion.

On Lorenzo's death in 1492, his son Piero took his place. Loutish and devoid of taste, Piero was totally unworthy of the Medici name; he only lasted two years. When Charles VIII of France invaded Italy in alliance with the Duke of Milan, Piero first opposed them but then, as it became clear that the French were winning, suddenly changed sides. He had to accept humiliating settlement terms. The Florentine people were so enraged that they drove him from the city and set up a republic. It was at this time that Niccolò Machiavelli, author of *The Prince*, held office in Florence, gaining first-hand experience in the art of intrigue and diplomacy.

The spiritual force behind the new republic was a fanatical Dominican friar by the name of Girolamo Savonarola (1452–98). During Lorenzo's last years, he had preached regularly in the Duomo. Audiences of thousands heard him inveigh against the excesses of the Medici and their entourage, prophesying apocalyptic punishments for the city if its people did not turn back to a godlier life. In 1494, he decreed a burning of "vanities", and Florentines rich and poor rushed to Piazza della Signoria with armfuls of books, jewellery, cosmetics and paintings which they hurled upon a huge bonfire in the middle of the square. A repentant Botticelli also joined the crowd, flinging some of his own paintings into the flames. However, Savonarola had powerful enemies within and without Florence (the notorious Borgia pope, for one) who soon brought about his downfall. Arrested, he was sentenced to death for heresy and, ironically, was hanged and burnt on the very spot where the "burning of vanities" had taken place only four years earlier.

In 1512, Piero's two brothers, Giovanni and Giuliano, returned, putting an end to the 18-year-old republic. Michelangelo's Medici tombs in San Lorenzo (one of which is for Giuliano) and his superb Laurentian Library date from this period. Expelled again in 1527, the persistent Medici were back three years later—after a dramatic eight-month siege of

Burning of Savonarola (1498) as seen by a contemporary artist.

Florence—with the help of the Holy Roman Emperor, Charles V.

During the subsequent rule of Duke Cosimo I de' Medici from 1537 to 1574, a rather heavy-handed attempt was made to revive the spirit of the earlier Medicean golden age. Some of Florence's most prominent monuments, the Santa Trinita Bridge, the Boboli Gardens, the Neptune Fountain in the Piazza della Signoria, Cellini's magnificent bronze *Perseus* in the Loggia dei Lanzi, date from this period.

A New Role

Florence now sank into a torpor for over three centuries under the rule of the boring Grand Dukes of Tuscany (Medici until 1743, Habsburg up to 1859). However, Anna Maria Ludovica, last of the Medici

Neptune fountain erected by the Medici on Piazza della Signoria.

line, made a final gesture worthy of her Renaissance forebears. Far-sightedly, she bequeathed the entire Medici art treasure to the city "to attract foreigners" and on condition that none of it ever be removed or sold. And foreigners came, a small but steady trickle of privileged, moneyed young men on the Grand Tour—the 18th-century finish to a gentleman's education.

In the 19th century a new species came, the "Italianate Englishman", led by the poets Byron and Shelley, and followed by the Brownings, John Ruskin and the Pre-Raphaelites. Rapturous Englishmen came or settled there in droves, bringing in their wake French, German and even Russian tourists. Queen Victoria herself visited the city, and Florence Nightingale—named after the city—was born there (see her statue, lamp and all, in Santa Croce cloister).

After the dramatic events of the Risorgimento, Italy's national movement to eject the Austrian occupant and unify the country, the city had a brief moment of glory as temporary capital of the new kingdom of Italy (1865–71). With the capital's permanent transfer to Rome, Florence's story merges into Italian history.

The 20th Century

Despite the excitement at the time of the unification, democracy failed to become firmly established in Italy. Crisis followed crisis, and people lost confidence in the government. During the First World War, Italy fought on the side of Britain and France against Germany and Austria, but afterwards she felt she had been insufficiently rewarded for her sacrifices. As parliamentary democracy disintegrated, Benito Mussolini's fascists seized power in 1922.

With the Rome–Berlin Axis of 1937, Mussolini linked the fate of Italy to that of Hitler's Germany, dragging his country into defeat in the Second World War. The Fascist government fell in 1943, and some of the most heroic battles of the Italian resistance were fought in and around Florence. Fortunately the city's unique art treasures survived.

Present-day Florence is an important, thriving business and university centre. Its vast new suburbs boast a variety of industries by no means all tourist orientated. Conscious heirs of a great creative tradition, today's Florentines keep their city in the forefront in the world of art, fashion and artisan crafts.

What to See

Unless you're on a package tour where decisions are already made for you, it pays to be selective in Florence. Otherwise, you may end up needing another holiday. Florence is a city to be savoured, its finest monuments and works of art lingered over. Don't try to "cover" it all if you're only here for a few days.

To ease your way, we've divided up the city into five geographical areas and described the most interesting sights within them. Each district can be covered on foot (cars, anyway, are banned from the historic centre).

But before exploring on your own, get the feel of the city by investing in a conducted coach tour. Inexpensive, three-hour morning and afternoon tours which provide a good overview of Florence can be arranged through your hotel.

Florence's museums and galleries are overwhelming: there are nearly 70, most of them worth visiting. We've noted the more important ones; which you visit will depend on your time and interests. If you've only a few days, better to see two or three at leisure than the lot at a gallop.

Make sure to check with your hotel on the current opening hours and closing days of museums. They're constantly changing.

Florence's churches are best seen and enjoyed in the context of the squares and streets and the life going on around them. On scorching summer afternoons you'll find their interiors a cool refuge and a welcome break from street and museum. But remember, they're places of worship, and shorts and halters are frowned upon.

Officially there are 24 historic churches in Florence, including the Duomo and Baptistery. You probably won't have time to visit a quarter of them, yet all boast architecture, memorials and art treasures of note. Wealthy merchant families vied with one another, and with the Medici, endowing and decorating chapels in their favourite churches, outdoing one another in lavishness and keeping quantities of artists and craftsmen busy for hundreds of years.

Some of the major churches —through which you're free to wander at will—have coin-operated sound-guides with good commentaries in different languages on the church's history and treasures.

The Florence Experience,

Piazzale Michelangelo offers the finest view in town: you can look over the full sweep of the city, from San Miniato to the Duomo and beyond.

screened hourly on the hour in the Cinema Edison on Piazza della Repubblica, provides a fine introduction to the city's past in 45 minutes of multivision.

Ponte Vecchio has linked city's two banks for almost 700 years.

Florence's streets are not wide, but their straight, right-angled pattern in its historic centre is a unique example of civilized town planning at a time when even Paris and London were a maze of twisting lanes and alleyways. The one street in central Florence that actually bends (Via Bentaccordi) only does so because it followed the horseshoe-shaped outer wall of the ancient Roman amphitheatre! On a map you can easily follow the line of the old city walls. Pulled down in the 19th century, they were replaced by broad but uninteresting tree-lined residential avenues or *viali*. Some of the original gates still stand forlornly in the middle of huge open squares.

The street names in Florence tell their own story: Via delle Terme (street of the baths) did have real Roman baths, and Via del Campidoglio (street of the capitol) boasted a great temple to Jupiter. Via degli Speziali (street of the spice merchants), Via dei Saponai (of the soap-makers), Corso dei Tintori (of the dyers) were once exclusively occupied by the particular trades. Only their names survive today, but Via de' Calzaiuoli (of the stocking- and shoemakers) is still *the* street for shoes.

FLORENCE

From the Duomo to the Uffizi

Duomo

Officially known as Santa Maria del Fiore (Our Lady of the Flower), the green, white and pink marble-faced Duomo was intended by city-proud Florentines as a cathedral to end all cathedrals (it can hold over 20,000 people!).

The great architect Arnolfo di 24 Cambio designed the Duomo.

Work began around 1296 on the site of a far smaller 5th-century church but was not completed until the second half of the 15th century. Its front remained unfaced until the 19th century.

Like most Tuscan churches of the time, the Duomo presents a uniquely local version

Of Crests and Such

Heraldry enthusiasts will find plenty to keep them busy in Florence. Coats of arms of families, trade guilds, city wards, and justices embellish numerous streets and even churches.

The most famous, of course, is the six balls of the Medici. These are said to represent pills, for the Medici, whose name means "doctors", were originally members of the guild of spice merchants and apothecaries. Five balls are coloured red, but the top ball is blue and bears the golden lily of France (a gift from Louis XI of France in the 15th century).

If the Medici coat of arms looks familiar to you, it may be through power of association: the pawnbroker's symbol evolved from it.

The Duomo's majestic cupola rises high above Florence, known from its crest as the city of the lily.

of Gothic, not easily compared with English or French ecclesiastical architecture of the same period.

The mighty **cupola** is a contribution from the Renaissance. First and unquestionably greatest of his talented peers, the architect Filippo Brunelleschi (1377–1446) had marvelled at the dome on Rome's Pantheon, rebuilt for Emperor Hadrian about A.D. 125. No one had subsequently achieved such an engineering feat.

The ambitious Florentines wanted to have a dome on their cathedral. In a public competition held in 1418, Brunelleschi submitted the winning design and a workable building scheme. (You can see his original wooden model in the Museo dell'Opera di Santa Maria del Fiore, see p. 30.) In Florence, where beauty and art were never the preserve of the rich alone, these competitions caused immense popular excitement. Citizens rich and

poor, high or low, often sat together on the juries.

Virtually completed in 1434, the marvellous dome—the first giant cupola since antiquity—was visible for miles around, confirming proud feelings that nothing was beyond a Renaissance man's ingenuity and science, especially a Florentine's. Its 138-foot diameter surpasses the domes of the Pantheon, St. Peter's in Rome, and St. Paul's in London. Climb to the top of its lantern and enjoy yet more breathtaking **panoramic views.**

Most of the original interior and exterior statuary of the Duomo was long ago removed to the Museo dell'Opera di Santa Maria del Fiore. There

Contrasting views—from and of the elegant Campanile by Giotto.

are nevertheless some important works of art on view in the cathedral. Make sure to take a look at Lorenzo Ghiberti's **bronze shrine,** below the high altar, made for the remains of St. Zenobius (one of Florence's first bishops). The Duomo's round stained-glass windows were also designed by the versatile Ghiberti.

Left of the entrance you'll spot unusual *trompe l'œil* frescoed "monuments" to two 15th-century *condottieri* (mercenary captains) who fought in Florentine pay. The right-hand one, painted by a master of perspective, Paolo Uccello, commemorates an Englishman, John Hawkwood, the only foreigner buried in the Duomo.

If you're lucky enough to be in Florence on Easter Sunday, don't miss the famous, centuries'-old Scoppio del Carro ceremony with its added costume pageantry in front of the Duomo. Fireworks on a decorated cart in the piazza are set off by an artificial dove pro-

genius Giotto. It's worth the 414-stair climb to the top and the entrance fee for a highly unusual bird's-eye **view** of the cathedral and the city.

Il Battistero (Baptistery)
Worth leaving till last, this precious gem of Romanesque architecture was built in the early 12th century on the site, traditionally, of a Roman temple of Mars. It served for a time as Florence's cathedral. Salvaged Roman columns were used in its construction. The exterior of the Baptistery remains as it was in the time of Dante.

Byzantine-style, 13th-century **mosaics** inside the cupola include scenes from the *Creation, Life of St. John* and a *Last Judgement.*

The Baptistery's tourist popularity rests on its three sets of bronze doors: those on the south side are by a 14th-century artist, Andrea Pisano; those on the north and east sides were made by Ghiberti in the first half of the 15th cen-

bronze models in the Bargello (p. 60), and judge for yourself. Facing the Duomo are the east doors, called the **Doors of Paradise** by an admiring Michelangelo. The name has stuck ever since. Between the little heads and Old Testament figures of the ten main panels, a proud Ghiberti set his own self-portrait. It's on the left door, two panels from the bot-

Scene from John the Baptist's life on Baptistery's south door.

tom, on the right. If you want to study the doors at close quarters, lunchtime or very late afternoon are best.

The simplest landmarks can hide the most dramatic events: the column standing on its own behind the Baptistery commemorates a tree that burst into bloom when the remains of a Florentine bishop, St. Zenobius, were carried past one wintry day centuries ago.

Piazza del Duomo and Piazza San Giovanni

Effectively two piazzas-in-one, this is undoubtedly Florence's religious hub for tourists. Opposite the Baptistery, see the graceful 14th-century Loggia del Bigallo, once part of the headquarters of a society for the care of orphans. On the same side of the piazza lies the seat of Florence's oldest, most respected social institution, the Brotherhood of the Misericordia (mercy). Every day and at most hours, you'll see black-frocked figures dashing out of its doors and roaring off in ambulance vans. They could be going to collect a sick child or comfort a dying old woman. This amazing democratic institution was thought up by the Florentines over 600 years before the existence of the Red Cross or Social Securi-

ty. Its members, unpaid volunteers from every walk of life, work on rotating shifts round the clock. They now run, among other things, Florence's emergency ambulance service.

Museo dell'Opera di Santa Maria del Fiore (Piazza del Duomo, 9) is the Duomo's own museum, where some of its most precious treasures and original sculptures are kept. See a magnificent 14th-15th-century silver-faced altar from the Baptistery; rich gold and silver reliquaries (one boasting the index finger of St. John); and Brunelleschi's original wooden model for the Duomo cupola. Don't miss Donatello's **Mary Magdalen statue**— a harrowing apparition; or his unforgettable **sculptured choir loft** (cantoria), full of movement and grace. Luca della Robbia's cantoria facing it is just as captivating. Here, too, is Michelangelo's unfinished **Pietà**; it is said that he intended it for his own tomb (See p. 118 for museum opening hours.)

In **Firenze com'era**, "Florence as it was" (Via dell'Oriuolo, 4), you will find paintings prints and photographs re

Take a sightseeing break in an unrivalled setting—in front of the Duomo (Santa Maria del Fiore)

tracing the city's physical history. The museum was formerly a monastery.

On the way down Via de' Calzaiuoli to the river you pass **Orsanmichele,** probably the only dual-purpose church in the world. The ground floor was designed for worship, the two upper floors for storing the city's grain reserve. In the church's ceiling you'll be shown the ducts down which grain was poured into waiting sacks below. Mystical and mysterious, the pillared interior is dominated by Orcagna's bulky but splendid 14th-century altarpiece, built around a miracle-working picture of the Madonna.

Adopted by the city's merchant and craft guilds, the church's plain, square, silo-like exterior, was embellished with Gothic-style niches and statues in the late 14th and early 15th centuries. Each guild paid for one of 14 niches and commissioned a statue of its patron or favourite saint for it. On the north side of the church stands Donatello's *St. George* (a copy: the original is in the Bargello, see p. 59). Commissioned by the armourers' guild, this was one of the first great statues of the Renaissance.

Ghiberti statues of *St. Matthew* and *St. Stephen* can be

seen on the side of the building facing the 13th-century Palazzo dell'Arte della Lana. Glance up at the impressive upper floors *(Saloni)*, reached via an overhead walkway from this *palazzo,* once the headquarters of the all-powerful wool-merchants' guild. The views alone are worth the climb.

Piazza della Signoria

If the Piazza del Duomo is Florence's religious heart, this is certainly its civic heart. When you first come upon it you'll be amazed at its sheer size, and at the cyclopean dimensions of the piazza.

Tourist attractions abound here—the *palazzo* itself; the Uffizi; a wealth of statuary, to say nothing of open-air cafés. And if you can't get to Venice, don't be disappointed: flocks of tame Florentine pigeons and professional photographers with bags of grain are on hand to make up for it. Some years the piazza serves as the setting on June 24, St. John's Day, for the Giuoco del Calcio, a highly colourful, traditional pageant and soccer (football) game in 16th-century costume (Recently, it's been held in the Boboli Gardens.) You should check with your hotel for details of the current year. Repeat performance on June 28

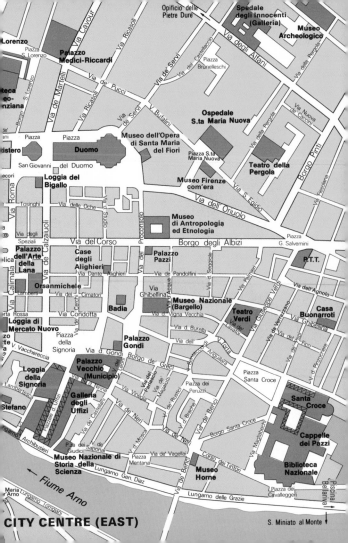

Opificio delle
Pietre Dure

Spedale
degli Innocenti
(Galleria)

Museo
Archeologico

LORENZO

Piazza
S. Lorenzo

Palazzo
Medici-Riccardi

Ospedale
S.ta Maria Nuova

TECA
EONZIANA

Piazza
Brunelleschi

Piazza

Duomo

Museo dell'Opera
di Santa Maria
del Fiori

Piazza S.ta
Maria Nuova

San Giovanni
del Duomo

Teatro della
Pergola

Loggia del
Bigallo

Museo Firenze
com'era

Via dell'Oriuolo

Tosinghi

Museo
di Antropologia
ed Etnologia

Piazza
G. Salvemini

Via del Corso

Borgo degli Albizi

Via degli
Speziali

Palazzo
dell'Arte
della
Lana

Case
degli
Alighieri

Palazzo
Pazzi

P.T.T.

Via di Pandolfini

Via dell'Agnolo

Orsanmichele

Via Dante Alighieri

Lamberti

Via
Ghibellina

Museo Nazionale
(Bargello)

Teatro
Verdi

Casa
Buonarroti

Porta Rossa

Badia

Vigna Vecchia

Loggia di
Mercato Nuovo

Via Condotta

Palazzo
Gondi

V. Vaccherecia

Piazza
della
Signoria

Borgo dei Greci

Piazza
Santa Croce

Palazzo
Vecchio
(Municipio)

Loggia
della
Signoria

Piazza dei
Peruzzi

Santa
Croce

Galleria
degli
Uffizi

Stefano

Cappelle
dei Pazzi

Museo Nazionale di
Storia della
Scienza

Piazza
Mentana

Biblioteca
Nazionale

Museo
Horne

Piazza dei
Cavalleggeri

Fiume Arno

Lungarno Gen. Diaz

Piscina
Bellariva

Maria
Arno

Lungarno delle Grazie

CITY CENTRE (EAST)

S. Miniato al Monte

Un-medieval in size at a time when only cathedrals were given monumental treatment, the fortress-like Palazzo della Signoria was undertaken at the same time as the Duomo—part of a mammoth public building programme. Designed by Arnolfo di Cambio, the Duomo's architect, this future seat of the cal, if unusual reason for this: the area around the 16th-century Neptune Fountain was formerly the site of the Uberti *palazzo*. One of Florence's leading 13th-century Ghibelline families, and one of the most hated, the Uberti were expelled *en masse* from the city, their palace razed to the ground and

city's government (it's still Florence's city hall) went up rather quickly. It was completed in 1314, 120 years before the Duomo.

Its off-centred, 308-foot-high tower helps soften the structure's stony squareness and echoes its off-centre position in the piazza. There's a practi-

Students at Italy's second oldest university confer; right, Giambologna's Rape of the Sabines.

its site officially cursed for all eternity. The Palazzo della Signoria stands just clear of this tainted land!

34

The equally famous **Loggia della Signoria,** or Loggia dei Lanzi, was built in the late 14th century. At first a covered vantage point for city officials at public ceremonies, it took its name later from Cosimo I's Germano-Swiss Landsknechts, or mercenaries, who used it as an open-air guardroom during his nine-year residence in the *palazzo.* When Cosimo moved to the Pitti in 1549, the Palazzo della Signoria became known as the Palazzo Vecchio, the "old palace"; the Landsknechts also moved on, but the Loggia's name stuck.

The first of its celebrated statuary, Cellini's fine bronze *Perseus,* was lodged here on Cosimo's order in the early 1550s; the two Giambologna works *(Rape of the Sabines* and *Hercules and the Centaur)* were added towards the end of the century, while the Roman statues at the back were 18th-century Medici additions.

A masterly feat of bronze-casting, the **Perseus** came within an inch of disaster. Cellini himself, in his lively autobiography, describes the agonizing moments when he had to throw all his pewter vessels into the molten metal—200 plates, goblets and pots—to keep it pouring smoothly into the mould.

And those beautiful little figures embellishing the statue's base might not have been there today if Cosimo's wife Eleonora of Toledo had had her way. Coveting them for herself, she badgered and cajoled Cellini for them. But he, with an eye perpetually cocked on public acclaim, ensured their destiny by soldering them firmly onto the base.

All this statuary was part of Cosimo's ambitious decoration scheme for the piazza, including his own bronze equestrian statue by Giambologna and the massive Neptune Fountain by Ammannati. He'd even toyed with a typically grandiose Michelangelo suggestion to extend the Loggia dei Lanzi round the entire piazza.

Statuary had always stood on the raised stone platform running the length of the *palazzo*'s façade. A *marzocco*, Florence's heraldic lion bearing the city's arms, has been there almost as long as the *palazzo* itself. Donatello's bronze *Judith and Holofernes* (now preserved within the palace) was transferred from the Medici Palace in 1494; Mi-

Today's young artists strive in the shadow of old Uffizi masters.

Davids Galore

The number of Davids in Florence is no coincidence. A favourite theme with shrewd politicians, artists and the common people, everybody liked to think of Florence as beautiful, young, fearless and divinely ordained for greatness, overcoming her worst enemies as David overcame Goliath.

The Medici commissioned Donatello's bronze *David* for their palace courtyard. Puritanical Savonarola himself didn't hesitate later to have this disturbingly erotic statue moved to the Palazzo della Signoria's courtyard where Verrocchio's bronze *David* already graced a staircase. And Michelangelo's giant *David* was commissioned as a morale-booster for the city —which it undoubtedly was.

chelangelo's *David* had been there since 1504. Sculpted in just two years out of a giant block of marble on which an earlier artist had made a clumsily unsuccessful start, *David* was moved to the Accademia in 1873 (see p. 52) and replaced by a copy. The present version is a second copy set up this century. The rather grotesque statue of *Hercules and Cacus* balancing it was done. by a **37**

16th-century sculptor, Baccio Bandinelli. He was also responsible, among other things, for the seated statue of Cosimo I's father in Piazza San Lorenzo.

The platform *(aringhiera)* served for public speakers or proclamations. A commemorative stone marks the exact spot where Savonarola was executed (see p. 16–17).

The elaborately ornate courtyard of the **Palazzo Vecchio,** or Palazzo della Signoria, comes as a surprise after the austerely medieval exterior. (See section on MUSEUM HOURS on p. 118.) This was part of a 16th-century scheme by Vasari to brighten the place up for his Medici masters. Verrocchio's bronze *putto* (cherub) fountain was specially brought from Lorenzo de' Medici's Careggi villa, as a final softening touch (the original is inside).

Before entering the Palazzo Vecchio, take a look at the right-hand wall close to the corner of the building: you'll see a man's profile cut into one of the lower stones. It's said to have been chiselled in minutes by Michelangelo—working "blind" with his hands behind his back, as a bet! And those dusty old stone lions in the *palazzo's* gloomy rear courtyard are reminders that real ones were once kept there, live symbols of Florence's heraldic lion, the *marzocco,* standing on the piazza outside.

The *palazzo's* highlights include the massive first-floor **Salone dei Cinquecento.** Built in 1496 for Savonarola's short-lived republican Council of 500, it was turned into a grand throne-room by Cosimo I, adorned with giant Vasari frescoes of Florentine victories and Michelangelo's *Victory* statue in a niche. Three centuries later, the first Italian national parliament sat here.

Just off the hall, don't miss the Vasari-designed **Studiolo,** a little gem of a study covered from floor to barrel-vaulted ceiling with painted allegorical panels (some on slate), and two Bronzino portraits of Cosimo I and his consort gazing haughtily down.

The Hall of Leo X (now offices) is frescoed with heroic Medicean themes. On the second floor are the apartments of Eleonora of Toledo (Cosimo I's wife), a riot of gilt, painted ceilings and rich furnishings. Note the frescoes imitating mosaics in the small chapel.

Visit the nearby 15th-century **Sala dei Gigli** (Hall of the Lilies), all blues and golds, lavishly decorated with Florentine heraldry, fine gilt-panelled ceiling, bright Ghirlandaio frescoes and doors superbly inlaid with figures of Dante and Petrarch.

In the next room, see a coloured bust of a lifelike, witty-looking Machiavelli, and Verrocchio's cuddlesome cherub at close quarters; then the splendid **Guardaroba,** a cupboard-lined room whose panels were painted in the 1570s with 53 maps of Tuscany and the four continents by two learned and artistic Dominican friars. Medici treasures were once stored here.

A dizzying gallery above the Salone connects with the Quartiere degli Elementi, another set of apartments. Don't miss the loggia and its breathtaking views of San Miniato and the Belvedere.

If you've time, climb up to the gallery below the battlements and, a little higher, to the top of the tower itself. Some 300 feet from the ground, you're treated here to one of the most sensational **panoramas** in all Florence. See also the small cell where Savonarola was locked up awaiting his execution in the piazza below.

To the *palazzo*'s right, the Uffizi museum stretches in a long U-shape right up to the Arno. Built in the second half of the 16th century by Vasari on Cosimo's order, the building was intended as headquarters for all the various government offices (hence the name), as the official mint and even as workshops for Medici-employed craftsmen. It's now one of the world's most famous art museums.

The Uffizi

A room a day, they say, is the way to see the Uffizi. Most tourists have a morning or even less to do it in. (See p. 118 for the museum's hours and closing days.)

Paintings, in chronological order, cover the cream of Italian and European art from the 13th to the 18th century. To avoid coming away with a blurry impression of the museum, feel no qualms about skipping over some of the 37 or so rooms that lead off two long, glassed-in galleries. Decorated with Roman statuary and sumptuous 16th-century Flemish tapestries, the galleries enjoy unique views over the Arno and Ponte Vecchio.

Start with those early Tuscan "greats", Cimabue and Giotto. In their altarpieces depicting enthroned madonnas **39**

tive, and the melancholy Filippo Lippi (1406–69). In the realm of religious art the outstanding painters were Fra Angelico (1387–1455), noted for the purity of line and colour, Leonardo's teacher Andrea Verrocchio (1435–88), also a fine sculptor, Domenico Ghirlandaio (1449–94), famous for his frescoes, the exquisitely lyrical Botticelli (1444–1510) and Filippino Lippi (c. 1457–1504).

Florentine painting rose to new heights in the 16th century with the versatile artist and scientist Leonardo da Vinci (1452–1519), the magnificent Michelangelo (1475–1564)—sculptor, architect, painter and poet—and Raphael (1483–1520), the epitome of classicism.

The great names in Florentine architecture were Giotto, Brunelleschi (1377–1446), Alberti (1404–72) and Michelozzo (d. 1472); the leading sculptors Lorenzo Ghiberti (1378–1455), Donatello (1386–1466), Luca della Robbia (1400–82), the specialist in terra cottas, and Benvenuto Cellini (1500–71), who excelled as a goldsmith as well.

Florentine Art in a Nutshell
Moving away from the Byzantine tradition, Giovanni Cimabue (1240–1302) founded the Florentine school, but it was Giotto (1266–1337), introducing naturalism, who made Florence the first city of Italian art.

The Renaissance was ushered in by Masaccio (1401–28), with his solid well-modelled human figures, followed by Andrea del Castagno (1423–57) and Paolo Uccello (1397–1475), master of perspec-

You can retrace the development of Florentine art, starting with Giotto (above), in Uffizi Gallery.

(painted in 1280 and 1310), the mosaic-like stiffness of Cimabue's work contrasts with Giotto's innovating depth and more expressive, realistic figures.*

Greatest painter of the important 14th-century Sienese school was Simone Martini: see the graceful *Annunciation* that he painted for Siena cathedral. And of all the later Italian Gothic masterpieces, Gentile da Fabriano's *Adoration of the Magi* (1423) is the most exquisite.

Nearby, don't miss Masaccio's *Madonna and Child with St. Anne,* an early Renaissance breakthrough because of its new "realism". Enjoy Fra Angelico's *Coronation of the Virgin,* full of light and music; and Paolo Uccello's *Battle of San Romano* (1456), an astounding exercise in perspective and volume. Originally three panels (the others are in Paris and London), they once hung in Lorenzo the Magnificent's bedroom. See also Piero della Francesca's powerful *Duke of Urbino,* warts and all.

Best loved and most reproduced among Renaissance paintings are Botticelli's haunting *Primavera* (spring) and the renowned *Birth of Venus.* Venus is said to represent "la bella Simonetta" Vespucci, mistress of luckless Giuliano de' Medici. Botticelli's lifelike but theatrical *Adoration* features Medici family portraits—Cosimo the Elder, his son Piero the Gouty, grandsons Lorenzo and Giuliano (smugly standing on the extreme left, a few years before his murder). Botticelli himself, in a yellow cloak, gazes out on the far right.

Outstanding among the 15th-century Flemish paintings is Hugo van der Goes' huge *Adoration of the Shepherds* triptych, which was painted in 1478 for the Medici's Flemish agent Tommaso Portinari. The kneeling Portinari are immortalized on its side-panels. In a sunnier, lighter vein is Ghirlandaio's *Adoration* (1487).

One room belongs to Leonardo da Vinci. See the *Baptism of Christ,* painted with his great teacher, Verrocchio. Only the background and left-hand angel were 18-year-old Leonardo's work, but enough, so the story goes, for Verrocchio to swear never to paint again. The exquisite *Annunciation,* painted around the same time, is entirely Leonardo's work, like his barely begun but dramatic *Adoration.*

---

*Because the rooms are rearranged fairly often, we have not given any numbers.

The octagonal Tribuna room, a 1589 Medici extension, symbolizes the four elements; its cupola is encrusted with mother-of-pearl representing water. The superb 17th-century inlaid stone table, specially made for the room, took 16 years to complete! See also Bronzino's portrayals of Cosimo I's Spanish wife *Eleonora of Toledo*, and his chubby smiling baby son—one of the most endearing child portraits ever painted.

The nude marble Medici *Venus,* excavated at Hadrian's Tivoli villa is thought to be a copy of a 4th-century B.C. Greek original by Praxiteles. Said to represent Phryne, notorious Athenian courtesan, it was apparently Thomas Jefferson's favourite statue, for he had a copy of it in his study!

Botticelli's renowned Birth of Venus, *commissioned to decorate the Medici's villa at Castello.*

Among German masterpieces in the Uffizi, don't miss Dürer's *Portrait of His Father* and *Adoration of the Magi*; and Cranach's life-like little portraits of *Luther*, his renegade-nun wife and a solidly Germanic *Adam and Eve*.

In the 15th-century Venetian school, be sure to look for Bellini's strange, dream-like *Sacred Allegory* (about 1490).

There is only one work by the great Michelangelo in the Uffizi: a round panel, the *Holy Family,* firmly but humanly treated, his earliest known painting (1503).

Equally notable are Raphael's placid, maternal *Madonna of the Goldfinch* and a wistful self-portrait done in Florence when only 23. In Titian's room, see his voluptuous *Venus of Urbino*.

Not to be missed is Rubens' *Portrait of his Wife*. She is so glowingly alive it's sad to think she died a year after it was painted.

The Niobe Room, built to accommodate Greco-Roman statuary in the centre, is grandly 18th century. Look for two delightful pictures of children by Chardin.

Some fine Dutch landscapes and Caravaggio's splendidly decadent *Bacchus* (1589) and Rembrandt's famous *Portrait of an Old Rabbi,* as well as two self-portraits, bring this orgy of great art to an end.

Stagger into the coffee-bar just beyond, and take a well-deserved drink and rest at an outside table above the Loggia dei Lanzi.

Renaissance art seen at its harmonious best in Raphael's self-portrait. Over a dozen members of the Medici family are buried in San Lorenzo.

From San Lorenzo to San Marco

San Lorenzo

Approached from Borgo San Lorenzo, the rough, unfaced stone façade of this church looks for all the world like a Tuscan barn. Michelangelo was supposed to complete it, but never got started, and, for once, 19th-century architects didn't try to finish the job.

Florence's first entirely Renaissance church and one of Filippo Brunelleschi's earliest architectural triumphs, the building was begun in 1419 on the site of a 4th-century church.

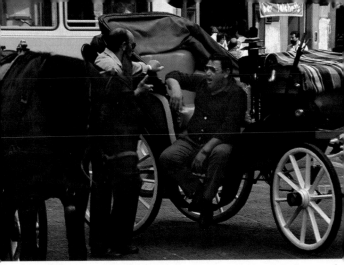

Medici money saw the project through, and Cosimo the Elder had his palace built within sight of San Lorenzo. The family arms ostentatiously adorn the ceiling.

The Medici are buried here in force. Cosimo the Elder himself is in the crypt, his father and mother in the Old Sacristy; Cosimo's two sons Piero the Gouty and Giovanni lie here, too, in a sumptuous bronze and porphyry tomb by Verrocchio; Piero's sons Lorenzo the Magnificent and the murdered Giuliano rest with their namesake cousins in Michelangelo's New Sacristy (see p. 47); the later Medici grand dukes are

See the town in style by horse and carriage—but negotiate fee first!

buried here also, as well as that giant of early Renaissance art, Donatello.

The uncluttered interior is a striking example—in an age of soaring Gothic—of new, exciting horizontal perspective effects achieved with the simplest means. Note the purity and elegance of those grey, classical *pietra serena* columns.

Cappelle Medicee (Piazza Madonna degli Aldobrandini; closed Sunday afternoons and Mondays). Once part of the Medici family church of San

Lorenzo but now separated from it, the **Cappella dei Principi** (Chapel of the Princes), a 17th-century Baroque extravaganza of multi-coloured, inlaid marble and semi-precious stones, was intended by Cosimo I as a family burial vault to end all burial vaults. The workmanship is astounding (it took three centuries to complete); the taste more doubtful. But Cosimo and family actually lie in the crypt.

The **New Sacristy** (*Sagrestia Nuova*) is what everybody *really* comes for. An amazing one-man show by Michelangelo who designed the interior and most of the sculptures; it took him more than 14 years.

Commissioned in 1520 by the future Pope Clement VII (illegitimate son of Giuliano de' Medici) as a worthy resting-place for his father and uncle Lorenzo the Magnificent, it was also to accommodate two recently-dead cousins (confusingly named Giuliano and Lorenzo).

The two more illustrious Medici are inconspicuously buried beneath Michelangelo's fine *Virgin and Child* statue, flanked by figures of Medici patron saints Cosmas and Damian (not by Michelangelo). The undistinguished cousins, ironically enough, have been immortalized by Michelangelo in two of the most famous funeral **monuments** of all time. On the right sits an idealized, warlike *Giuliano* above two splendid figures symbolizing Night and Day resting on the elegantly curved sarcophagus. The unfinished face of Day, with the visible marks of Michelangelo's chisel, somehow makes the figure all the more remarkable. Opposite, a thoughtful *Lorenzo* sits above *Dawn* and *Dusk*. The specially foreshortened effect of the upper windows give the cupola a feeling of still greater height. Statues and architecture produce an unforgettable impression.

To the left of the entrance to the church of San Lorenzo is another Michelangelo wonder, the **Biblioteca Mediceo-Laurenziana** (Laurentian Library). Commissioned by Pope Clement VII to house a precious collection of Medici books and manuscripts in 1524, opened to the public in 1571, it's probably one of the most beautiful libraries in the world. Closed Sundays.

It's hard to recapture the Medici atmosphere in the **Palazzo Medici-Riccardi** (Via Cavour, 1; closed Wednesdays), now Florence's Carabinieri-guarded prefecture. But rest awhile in a peaceful little walled **47** garden with orange trees behind the main courtyard. Then climb up to the tiny family chapel to see Benozzo Gozzoli's fresco, the *Procession of the Magi,* that covers its walls. Painted in 1459, in warm, rich colours, it's a lavish pictorial display of everybody who was anybody in Florence—including, of course, the whole Medici clan and their supporters. The chapel remains exactly as the 15th-century Medici knew it. The ground-floor museum of Mediciana features Lorenzo's death mask, some family portraits and other works of art.

In **Chiostro dello Scalzo**

(Cloister of the Bare-footed Order, Via Cavour, 69) are scenes from St. John's life frescoed in chiaroscuro technique by 16th-century painter Andrea del Sarto. Closed for restoration.

From *Last Supper* to *Resurrection,* the best frescoes of Andrea del Castagno (1423–57), a master of vigorous forms and colours, grace the refectory of **Cenacolo di Santa Apollonia** in a former Benedictine nunnery (Via XXVII Aprile, 1). Ring for admittance.

Museo di San Marco

An old monastery re-designed by the Medici palace architect, Michelozzo, and built for the Dominicans with Medici money in 1437, this is one of Florence's most evocative attractions. (See section on MUSEUM HOURS on p. 118.)

Fra Angelico (1387–1455) lived here as a monk, and most of his finest paintings and frescoes, including the great *Deposition* altarpiece, can be seen in this museum. Off the graceful, columned cloister with its venerable cedar tree, you'll find Angelico's luminous paintings; and, in the small refectory, a vivid Ghirlandaio mural of the *Last Supper*—a favourite subject for monastery eating rooms.

Upstairs, visit the simple monks' cells, each one frescoed for religious inspiration by Fra Angelico and his pupils. His famous *Annunciation* fresco

Variations on a devout theme—one of Fra Angelico's movingly simple Annunciation scenes in San Marco. **49**

is located in cell no. 3. At one end of the row of cells see the suite reserved for Cosimo de' Medici's meditations and, at the opposite end, that of the monastery's fiery prior and enemy of the Medici, Girolamo Savonarola. See his haunting portrait by fellow-monk Fra Bartolomeo, the religious banner he carried through Florence's streets and a painting of his execution on Piazza della Signoria.

Walk into Michelozzo's superbly proportioned colonnaded library and you'll be reminded of Fra Angelico's painted backgrounds.

The great bell placidly resting in the cloister has had a chequered career. Donated by Cosimo de' Medici and known as *la piagnona* ("great moaner"), Savonarola's puritanical supporters were nicknamed *i piagnoni* after it. It tolled to alert the monks when Savonarola's enemies came to arrest him. Spitefully condemned for this to 50 years' "exile" outside the city walls, the bell was whipped through the streets all the way to its new home.

Piazza Santissima Annunziata

Set in the most Renaissance of Florence's squares, the church

of **Santissima Annunziata** deserves to be savoured in the context of its surroundings. It's best approached from the Via de' Servi (named after the Servite Order for whom the church was rebuilt).

The entire piazza was probably designed by Brunelleschi when he built the Spedale degli Innocenti (see below). Medici money backed the scheme and the church's architect, Michelozzo, stuck to Brunelleschi's original vision, ensuring the piazza's lasting harmony. Even Giambologna's bronze equestrian statue of Grand Duke Ferdinando I (1608) and the two 17th-century fountains add to the unity of the square and the feeling of spaciousness.

Beyond the church's vestibule frescoed by Andrea del Sarto and others, and immediately left of the entrance, is the important 15th-century **shrine** of the Annunziata. It shelters an old fresco that is shown only on special feast days. Said to have miraculous properties, it's been the object of pilgrimages and votive offerings for centuries.

The unusual round choir survives from the 15th century, but many of the over-ornate interior decorations date from the late 17th century.

The **Galleria dello Spedale degli Innocenti** (Piazza Santissima Annunziata, 12) contains sculptures and paintings (15th to 16th century) belonging to this, Florence's foundling hospital, which was built to Brunelleschi's design in the early 1400s. Note the series of 15th-century glazed terracotta roundels of appealing swaddled babes by Andrea della Robbia on its arched façade. Closed Wednesdays.

One of Italy's most important museums housed in a former grand-ducal palace the **Museo Archeologico** (Via della Colonna) boasts major ancient Egyptian and Etruscan collections. Among its highlights, the famous 6th-century-B.C. Greek *François Vase;* two remarkable Etruscan bronzes, the *Chimera* and *Arringatore* (the orator); remnants of build-

Michelangelo's original David *holds centre-stage in the* Accademia.

ings from Roman Florence. The wonderfully reconstructed Etruscan tombs in its gardens were badly damaged in the 1966 flood. Closed Mondays.

Originally an art school founded by Cosimo I, the **Galleria dell'Accademia,** the exhibition hall (Via Ricasoli, 60), was added in the 18th century for the students' benefit. Its collection of 13th–16th century Florentine School paintings is second only to the Uffizi's. There are tapestries and fine furniture, like the typical Florentine painted marriage chests. (See section on Museum Hours on p. 118.)

The gallery also boasts seven major Michelangelo sculptures, including the original **David.** Brought here from the Piazza della Signoria in 1873 to preserve it from the elements, this David—unlike its copy—is truly impressive.

The **Conservatorio Musicale Luigi Cherubini** (Via degli Alfani, 80) has an important music library, with composers' original manuscripts and a unique collection of old musical instruments started by Grand Duke Ferdinando de' Medici in the 17th century.

Stroke its nose, throw a coin— and you'll return to Florence!

Mercato Nuovo to Santa Maria Novella

The main attraction of **Mercato Nuovo** (the Straw Market) are the stalls selling leather goods, straw baskets and what-have-you (see p. 86). But don't overlook the 17th-century bronze statue of a boar, known as *Il Porcellino* (the piglet).Tradition has it that if you stroke his nose and throw a coin into the fountain, you will be sure to return to Florence. In the centre of the market is a marble circle, the Batticulo (buttock smacker), where, in the 16th century, welchers and swindlers were soundly beaten.

In the **Palazzo Davanzati** (Via Porta Rossa, 9) you can see how wealthy medieval and Renaissance Florentines really lived. A 14th-century palace with a stern exterior, its rooms are full of colour. See the lavish 14th-century, patterned *trompe l'œil* frescoes (Sala dei Pappagalli) and 15th-century furniture and paintings recreating the atmosphere of each room. Everything from toilets to kitchens, not forgetting amusing graffitti on some of the walls.

On the way to Piazza Santa Trinita, discover one of Florence's most unassuming churches, **Santi Apostoli,** situated on the Piazza del Limbo. Legend has it that Charlemagne himself built it. Inside are some pieces of flint, taken from Jerusalem's Holy Sepulchre centuries ago by a crusader member of the Pazzi family. These are used to light the fireworks for the Scoppio del Carro on Easter Sunday (see p. 28).

After the late 16th-century façade, the Gothic interior of the fine church of **Santa Trinita** comes as a complete surprise. It was built between the 13th and 15th centuries on the site of a far older church whose remains are still visible.

Look for the late 15th-century Sassetti chapel (second on the right from the chancel chapel), with scenes of St. Francis' life by Ghirlandaio. Besides the donor and his family, Lorenzo the Magnificent and his sons are also portrayed against contemporary Florentine backgrounds.

The Strozzi, the Davanzati and the Gianfigliazzi lived in the area and endowed richly frescoed chapels here. So did the Bartolini-Salimbeni family, whose exquisite, early 16th-century *palazzo* (now the French consulate) faces the church, and the Spini family, whose fortress-like 13th-century residence (now Palazzo

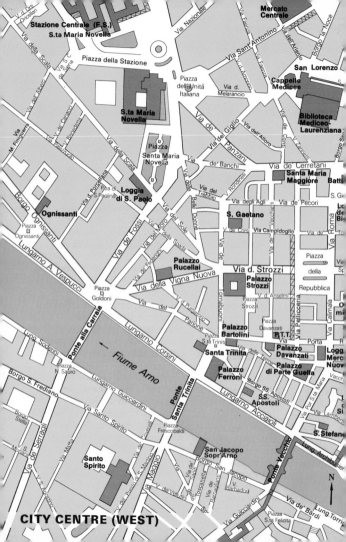

CITY CENTRE (WEST)

Ferroni) stands at the corner of the piazza. The 15th-century **Palazzo Strozzi,** one of the most beautiful private residences in the whole of Florence, is nearby on Via de' Tornabuoni.

Out on the Piazza Santa Trinita stands the so-called Column of Justice. It is nothing of the kind, but rather a monument set up by Grand Duke Cosimo de' Medici to celebrate his victory over a band of exiled Florentines anxious to overthrow him and re-establish more democratic government.

Despite its fine 17th-century façade and the della Robbia glazed-terracotta relief over the doorway, **Ognissanti** (All Saints Church) actually dates from around 1250. Its builders, the Umiliati ("Humble Ones"), were an industrious monastic community who had a remarkably successful wool business. They were reputed to have been among the first to put Florence on the road to financial prosperity.

See Botticelli's *St. Augustine* and, in the refectory, the famous *The Last Supper* by Ghirlandaio, frescoes commissioned by the Vespucci family of wealthy merchants. Several family members are buried here, as indeed is Botticelli himself.

Florentines at Sea
Amerigo (1454–1512), most famous VESPUCCI of them all, went down in history as the man who gave his name to America. Banker, businessman and navigator, he crossed the Atlantic in Columbus' footsteps, touching the North American coast for the very first time. Columbus believed to the end he'd landed in Asia: Vespucci knew *he* had found a great new continent. America deserves his name.

Over 20 years later, yet another Florentine navigator, GIOVANNI DA VERRAZZANO, searching for the legendary North-West Passage to Asia discovered New York Bay.

Santa Maria Novella

One of Florence's greatest monastic churches, Santa Maria Novella was designed by Dominican architects in the mid-13th century. A Dominican community still resides in its precincts. An unlikely setting for the beginning and end of Boccaccio's *Decameron!*

The bold 15th-century inlaid marble front, begun in Gothic style a century earlier, was completed to Renaissance taste by architect Leon Battista Alberti, also responsible for the graceful Palazzo Rucellai nearby. The Medici *didn't* pay for this church, and the Rucellai donors—to make sure their generosity wouldn't go unnoticed—had their name put up in large Roman letters under the top cornice.

Walk through the mystic gloom of the 328-foot-long nave to a cluster of richly frescoed family chapels around the altar. See the chancel behind the altar with its *Scenes from the Lives of the Virgin and St. John* **frescoes** by Ghirlandaio and his pupils, paid for by the wealthy Tornabuoni family (coin-operated floodlamps illuminate them). Don't miss the splendidly inlaid wooden choir-stalls.

Ghirlandaio, Florence's top "social" painter in the late 15th century, peopled the frescoes with Tornabuonis—one of which was Lorenzo the Mag-

Obelisk in front of Santa Maria Novella was horse-race turnpost.

nificent's mother—all dressed in the latest fashions.

To the altar's right, a Strozzi family chapel colourfully frescoed by Filippino Lippi, son of the famous painter Fra Filippo; next to it a Bardi chapel with 14th-century frescoes. The Gondi chapel to the left of the altar contains a Brunelleschi altar **crucifix** (his answer to Donatello's "peasant" in Santa Croce; see p. 64); and, on the extreme left, a Strozzi chapel with 14th-century **frescoes** of

the *Last Judgement, Heaven* and *Hell*—its donors, of course, depicted in Heaven!

Most striking of all is Masaccio's **Trinity** (c. 1427) on the wall of the left aisle. Amazing for its uncanny spatial depth, the fresco sets the crucifixion, with kneeling husband-and-wife donors, in a purely Renaissance architectural setting, dramatically breaking away from everything that had been painted before. You'll quite likely see someone praying or lighting a votive candle in front of it, just as you may see and hear mass being said in one of those frescoed chapels. It's all part of the beauty of a city whose life, art and history are forever intertwined.

To the left of the church lie part of the surviving monastery buildings (nominal entry fee). The great 14th-century **cloister** with its three giant cypresses is a haven of tranquillity after the noisy piazza. From here you can admire the church's graceful 14th-century campanile at close range. Known as the Chiostro Verde, meaning green cloister for the tint of frescoes once painted here by Paolo Uccello, it leads to the refectory (where some detached surviving frescoes are now kept), to a smaller cloister and to the famous, impressively **57** vaulted chapter-house, the **Cappellone degli Spagnoli** (Spanish Chapel), named in honour of Cosimo I's Spanish wife, Eleonora of Toledo. Gigantic 14th-century frescoes cover its four walls. The artist incorporated a picture of the Duomo with cupola—60 years before its actual completion.

Votive altar in S. Maria Novella.

Bargello, Santa Croce and San Miniato

Museo Nazionale (Bargello)

This forbidding-looking fortress at Via del Proconsolo, 4 is to sculpture what the Uffizi is to painting. Florence's first city hall and one of its earliest public buildings (begun about 1250), it served as the seat of magistrates *(podestà)* responsible for law and order and

later housed the Captain of Justice *(bargello)*, 16th-century equivalent of a police commissioner.

Men were imprisoned, tortured and executed here. Its outer walls were decorated with life-like effigies of traitors and criminals hung by the neck or by one foot—horrific warnings to would-be wrongdoers, often by the best artists. Botticelli himself did the Pazzi conspirators in 1478.

The stern courtyard, softened by the brownish hues of its *pietra forte,* is covered with stone plaques bearing the arms of successive *podestà.* Just off it lies the **Sala Michelangelo e scultura Fiorentina del cinquecento** (Hall of Michelangelo and 16th-Century Florentine Sculptors). Note wall marks recording the 1966 flood level —9½ feet.

Michelangelo was 21 when he finished his early masterpiece *The Drunken Bacchus,* beautifully god-like but just a shade unsteady on his legs! He sculpted the marble *Virgin and Child (Pitti Tondo)* eight years later, while working on his famous *David.* And for a portrait of the artist, see Daniele da Volterra's bronze bust of Michelangelo at his sourest. Don't miss several Cellini bronzes, his handsome bust of Cosimo I de' Medici and the small bronze model for his *Perseus* in the Loggia dei Lanzi.

A 14th-century stone staircase leads to an arcaded loggia on the first floor, where you'll see Giambologna's bronze *Mercury* and his impressionistic series of bronze birds displayed along the parapet. All were garden or fountain decorations for the Medici.

The first floor holds sumptuous, largely Medici-owned collections, ranging from Italian and Tuscan ceramics and old Murano glass, to French Limoges enamels and astonishing sea-shells chiselled like cameos. In the 14th-century chapel's frescoes, painted by a pupil of Giotto, look for the sharp-featured man behind the kneeling figure on the right— supposedly Dante.

If you see nothing else, see the **Great Hall,** which contains the spirit of early Renaissance Florence. Donatello's sturdily human *St. George* (1416), embedded in a huge expanse of blank wall, dominates the high-vaulted room. Commissioned by the armourers' guild as their contribution to the exterior decorations of Orsanmichele (see p. 32), it's generally held to be the first great sculptural breakthrough of the Renaissance.

Donatello's bronze *David*, the first Renaissance nude statue, once graced the Medici palace courtyard. In contrast to the "modern" feeling of the *St. George*, *David* has an antique sensuality about it, while his delightful bronze *Amore* (cupid) is positively Roman in style. More personal and dramatic are the two marble versions of a youthful and an older *St. John the Baptist*.

Be sure to look at Ghiberti's and Brunelleschi's original bronze models *(The Sacrifice of Abraham)* for the Baptistery doors competition of 1401, clearly a close contest. Don't neglect several sensitive portrait busts of the marble and glazed terracotta reliefs of madonnas. Two of them by Luca della Robbia, white on blue ground, are purity itself.

On the second floor, see Verrocchio's bronze *David* (about 1471); his 19-year-old pupil Leonardo da Vinci is said to have been the model.

Opposite the Bargello you will see the church known as the **Badia Fiorentina,** with its graceful bell-tower part Romanesque, part Gothic. Go inside

Baptistery without the Ghiberti doors shown on old wedding chest.

for a moment to admire Filippino Lippi's delightful *Madonna Appearing to St. Bernard,* on the left as you enter.

Casa Buonarroti (Via Ghibellina, 70; see section on MUSEUM HOURS on p. 117) was bought by bachelor Michelangelo for his closest relatives. It contains letters, drawings, portraits of the great man, plus a collection of 17th-century historical paintings highlighting his long life.

See his famous sculptured relief, the *Madonna of the Staircase,* done before the artist was 16. His astonishing *Battle of Lapiths and Centaurs* dates from around the same time.

Santa Croce

With its vast expanse of open piazza, Santa Croce became one of the city's social and political hubs. Lorenzo and Giuliano de' Medici staged lavish jousts here; and half-starving but defiant Florentines turned out in force during the 1530 siege of their city to watch or take part in a special soccer game.

Santa Croce started off in 1228 as a modest chapel, erected in true Franciscan fashion right in the middle of a working district. Arnolfo di Cambio, the Duomo's architect, drew up the plans for a larger church, which was completed in the 14th century. Its interior is grandly Gothic; the façade, 19th-century Gothic.

Within are buried some of the most illustrious figures in Italian history. Biographer Vasari designed Michelangelo's tomb (first on the right-hand wall). Smuggled out of Rome in a packing-case, his body was given the finest funeral in Florentine memory. The seated statues on the monument represent Sculpture, Painting and Architecture—three domains in which he remains immortal.

The next tomb, Dante's, has no body, much to the Florentine's dismay. His real grave is in Ravenna where he died and **61** the Ravennese have never given in to Florentine pleas for its return. Further along you'll spot Machiavelli's (1469–1527) tomb. Civil servant, political theorist, historian and playwright, his book *The Prince*—advice on how to rule a state—has made his name, fairly or not, a synonym of hypocrisy and devilish cunning.

Further on lies a non-Florentine but a great Italian, Rossini (1792–1868), composer of the beautiful opera *The Barber of Seville*.

Opposite Michelangelo is the Pisan genius Galileo (1564 to 1642) who perfected the earliest astronomical telescope. On the same side lies Lorenzo Ghiberti, creator of the Baptistery doors.

As you walk around this great church, you'll be stepping over any number of fascinating 13th- and 14th-century tomb slabs set in the floor, their effigies badly worn but still visible. Santa Croce was always a popular burial place.

As you progress up the nave, take note of the splendid late 15th-century marble pulpit sculptures with scenes from the

The pure, geometric design of Brunelleschi's Pazzi chapel influenced early Renaissance style.

life of St. Francis and, further on the right, Donatello's sensitive *Annunciation* in grey *pietra serena*. See also a coloured wooden **Christ** on the cross by Donatello. His friend Brunelleschi mockingly called it "a peasant" (see p. 57).

The honeycomb of family chapels on either side of the high altar contains a wealth of frescoes from the 14th to the 16th centuries. Immediately to the right of the altar in the **Bardi Chapel,** you'll find Giotto's finest, most moving paintings: scenes from the life and death of St. Francis, done around 1320.

The adjoining chapel, containing Giotto frescoes of the life of St. John, belonged to the Bardis' partners, the Peruzzi, rich bankers who gave most of the money for the imposing sacristy. Not long afterwards the Peruzzi were ruined by Edward III of England's "bankruptcy" (see p. 14).

If the Pazzi family has an infamous reputation, it's more than redeemed by the small **chapel** bearing their name. One of the earliest, most exquisite Renaissance religious interiors, it was designed for the Pazzi family by Brunelleschi in 1430. Reached by an entry beside the church, you'll see it facing you across a cloister.

The Santa Croce museum contains frescoes and statues removed from the church, but its proudest treasure is Cimabue's massive 13th-century **painted cross,** almost destroyed in the 1966 flood.

Walk into the beautiful second cloister and try to imagine it with the flood waters so high you could only see the tops of its arches.

Museo della Fondazione Horne (Via de' Benci, 6; see p. 118 for museum's hours) is a superb little 15th-century palace, restored, lived-in and bequeathed to Florence in 1916 by an Englishman, H. P. Horne. Within you will see his priceless collection of paintings, drawings, sculptures, ceramics, furniture, coins and medals, and old household utensils.

The **Museo di Storia della Scienza** (Museum of the History of Science; Piazza dei Giudici, 1) has a fascinating collection of scientific instruments and unusual curiosities, from Galileo's telescopes and (preserved) middle finger to Torricelli's original "tube" and an Edison phonograph. A change from pure culture.

Green-and-white San Miniato is residence of Benedictine monks.

San Miniato and Piazzale Michelangelo

A pleasant walk or bus ride (No. 13 from Piazza dei Giudici) will take you up to the Piazzale Michelangelo with its incomparable **panoramic view** over the city and to the church of San Miniato nearby.

St. Miniato, an early Christian martyred in the 3rd century A.D., is said to have carried his severed head up here from Florence and set it down where the church was later built. All too-often neglected by tourists in a hurry, San Miniato is one of Florence's most romantic churches and a favourite for weddings.

Rebuilt in the early 11th century, it's a remarkable example of Florentine-style Romanesque architecture. The sight of its superb green and white marble façade glinting golden in the late afternoon sun is something you'll long remember.

The interior has all the splendour of a Byzantine basilica with its wealth of richly inlaid marble to its mosaic decorations. Note the extraordinary embroidery effect of the nave'

Admire yet another David while taking in the view from Piazzale

3th-century marble floor—a bit like the bridal train of some fairy-tale princess. See also the fine 15th-century chapel and tomb of the Cardinal of Portugal (who died in Florence), and some well-preserved 14th-century frescoes in the sacristy.

Relax awhile on the great terrace and enjoy the view. Or adjourn to the little shop-cum-bar run by resident Benedictine-Olivetans, where a charming, white-robed father will sell you anything from honey and herb liqueurs to a postcard or a coke.

If it weren't for Michelangelo, San Miniato might not be here today. During the 1530 siege, when the Emperor Charles V's Spanish gunners pounded away at the city, San Miniato was well within range and might have been blown to pieces. But Michelangelo, in charge of the Florentine defences, had a temporary fortress hastily built around the site, while protecting the bell tower with mattresses and wool bales. The fortress (now enclosing a cemetery) was later made permanent. A similar 16th-century fortification, the Forte Belvedere, can be seen to the left.

Pitti Palace to Santa Maria del Carmine

Cross over the Arno on the oldest bridge in Florence, **Ponte Vecchio,** the only one spared in the last war. The present construction, complete with overhanging boutiques, dates back to 1345. Vasari built the covered passageway above the shops

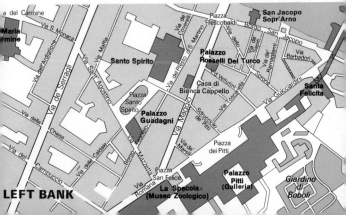

so that Grand Duke Cosimo Ie' Medici could go from the Pitti to the Uffizi without getting wet.

From the double terrace in the middle, admire the elegant, softly curved arches of **Ponte Santa Trinita.** Destroyed in 1944, the bridge was carefully reconstructed, exactly as Ammannati had built it in the 16th century.

Palazzo Pitti

Official Medici and grand-ducal residence since 1549, royal palace of united Italy from 1865 to 1871, it's another Florentine "must". The Pitti Palace comprises museums and galleries, plus some ten acres of ornate Italian gardens and many charming surprises. (All museum hours are listed separately on p. 118.)

In the sumptuous **Galleria Palatina,** you'll feel more like a collector's guest than a tourist. Priceless paintings hang four-high against a lavish gilt, stuccoed and frescoed décor. They've all been left just as the last Medici and later grand dukes placed them, according to personal preference rather than any historical sequence.

There are splendid works here by Botticelli, Raphael, Titian, Rubens, Velazquez and Murillo, exhibited in grandiose halls, some of which bear the names of their décor (the "Hall of the Iliad" has frescoed scenes from Homer's epic). If time is short, here's what not to miss.

Raphaels abound : make sure to see his *Pregnant Women,* his incisive portrait of *Cardinal Inghirami;* and the famous round painting, the *Madonna of the Chair.* The enigmatic, romantic *Veiled Woman* was, in fact, Raphael's mistress and favourite model.

The "Hall of Mars" is dominated by Rubens' powerful allegory the *Consequences of War,* one of the most striking 17th-century Baroque paintings. See also his *Four Philosophers,* with a ruddy-faced Rubens himself standing on the left.

Most memorable of several fine Titians are *The Magdalen,* the searching *Portrait of a Young Englishman* and *The Concert.*

Look for Fra Filippo Lippi's sensitive *Virgin and Child* (1452), the Virgin's own birth painted in the background.

Though each room is more heavily decorated than the last, Room 29, covered from floor to ceiling with 17th-century frescoes, tops them all for sheer extravagance.

In the 16 sumptuously decorated rooms of the **Museo degli Argenti** (Silverware Mu- **69** seum), admire some of the Medici's most cherished jewels, cameos, gold, silver, crystal and ivory objects, furniture and porcelain. Truly priceless is Lorenzo the Magnificent's personal collection of 16 exquisite vases in semi-precious stones. The room they're displayed in is the biggest surprise of all: its 17th-century architectural frescoes give you a dizzying, but perfect, optical illusion of extra height and depth; a red-cloaked Lorenzo appears in three of the allegorical murals.

The best of 19th- and 20th-century Italian art, especially Tuscan painting, can be seen in the **Galleria d'Arte Moderna** (Gallery of Modern Art). Discover the exciting Macchiaioli ("blotch-painters"), Tuscany's own Impressionist movement of the 1860s. Look out for paintings by Fattori and Signorini.

Museo delle Carrozze has two rooms of shiny, elegant state coaches. The **Appartamenti Monumentali** (Royal Apartments), a sort of mini-Versailles, were first inhabited by the Medici, later by Italy's royal House of Savoy.

The Palazzo della Meridiana at the south-west corner of the Pitti Palace is given over to the **Collezione Contini Bonacossi,** with its renowned old

master paintings, exquisite furniture and ceramics.

Entrance is free to the **Giardino di Boboli** (open daily 9 a.m. to 7 p.m. in summer), an Italian pleasure-garden of cypress- and hedge-lined alleys and arbours filled with unusual statuary, lodges, grottoes and fountains. Originally a quarry where the Pitti's huge stone blocks were extracted, the park was built for Cosimo I's nature-loving consort Eleonora of Toledo.

The Boboli's highlights include a deliciously fat, turtle-riding, marble dwarf, Cosimo I's court jester; the Grotta Grande (near the *palazzo*'s left entrance); the Amphitheatre and a fine glimpse of Florence; the Casino del Cavaliere housing the Museo delle Porcellane, a fine porcelain collection; the Vasca del Nettuno, and unique Piazzale dell'Isolotto, an idyllic island, fountain, greenery and statue ensemble.

Santo Spirito

A monastic church of the Augustinian order dating back to the 13th century, Santo Spirito was totally re-designed by Brunelleschi and built in the second half of the 15th century after his death.

From its unfinished, unusually bare, but dramatic exterior,

you'll step into a masterpiece of Renaissance architectural harmony. Thirty-eight elegant side altars line the walls, slender grey-stone columns with Corinthian capitals and an interplay of arches give the impression of tremendous depth. The adjoining cloister is a 17th-century effort.

Next to the church, in the original monastery refectory, see the impressive 14th-century frescoes of the *Last Supper* and *Crucifixion,* and the fine medieval and Renaissance sculptures of the **Museo della Fondazione Romano.**

The Augustinians once ran a hospital, where young Michelangelo came–with the assent of the prior–to perfect his knowledge of anatomy by dissecting the bodies of dead patients.

Santa Maria del Carmine

Mecca of artistic pilgrimage, this unpretentious church shelters some of the most momentous **frescoes** ever painted. Commissioned by the Brancacci family, Masaccio and his teacher Masolino worked from 1423 to 1427 on fresco decorations for their chapel here. Masolino's own work is striking enough but Masaccio's *Tribute Money* and the *Expulsion of Adam and Eve from the Garden of Eden* lift painting

to a completely new plane. His feeling for light and space, his dramatically stage-set figures, the concreteness of their forms are little short of an inspired miracle. Nothing of the kind had been painted before; the Renaissance had come to stay. Masaccio died at 27 before completing his commission. **71**

Florentine artists young and old arrived in never-ending streams to marvel at and learn from his work. Michelangelo himself came as a pupil to sketch the figures. It was here, so the story goes, that Pietro Torrigiani, a fellow-student, broke Michelangelo's nose, goaded by the latter's taunts at his clumsy copying. Torrigiani, fearing Medici retribution for damaging their young protégé, fled abroad, eventually ending up in London where he sculpted Henry VII's tomb in Westminster Abbey!

If Masaccio's paintings are miraculous, a miracle saved them from destruction when the church was gutted by fire in the 18th century. The Brancacci chapel and a small part of the main building were the only things saved.

Visit Fiesole's Roman ruins any time of day; a sunny morning is best for the Masaccio frescoes.

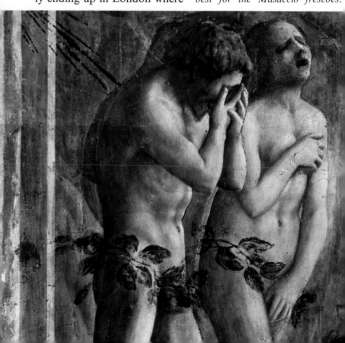

Excursions

Many travel agencies offer a wide choice of conducted or unconducted coach tours. The tourist office (see p. 122) also organizes several off-beat local tours—the finest Florentine villa gardens from April to June, nearby vineyards, farms and wine-cellars in September and October.

Regional and long-distance bus lines (see p. 123) cover the whole of Tuscany, while city buses are useful for shorter excursions. Here are a few suggestions less than an hour from Florence by car or bus.

Nearby Attractions

Reached by a winding, villa-bordered road, **Fiesole** (No. 7 bus from Piazza San Marco) is a refreshing little town, pleasant to explore or eat at in the evening, with wonderful views over Florence and the Arno Valley. This former Etruscan hill stronghold has a splendidly situated camping site.

If you can, stop off on the way to see the exquisite **Badia Fiesolana** (signposted to the left), originally Fiesole's cathedral, rebuilt with Medici money in the 15th century.

Apart from wall fragments, Fiesole bears hardly a trace of

the Etruscans, but the Roman ruins are impressive. Off the main piazza lies the well-preserved **Roman theatre.** Built around 100 B.C. and still in use today, it seats some 2,500 spectators. See the Roman bath and temple remains and a small but interesting Archaeological Museum.

Completed in the 13th century, **San Romolo** cathedral has a Byzantine atmosphere within. Its aggressively Tuscan stone turret, visible for miles around, dates back to 1213.

Don't miss a steep but picturesque walk (left of the main piazza) up to **San Francesco** church and its mini-monastery. The views on the way are memorable and the monastery, with its tiny, peaceful cloisters, enchanting.

If you've time, visit Fiesole's Museo Bandini for a well-dis-

Flowering gorse enlivens Tuscan tableau of greenery and vineyards.

played collection of furniture and 14th-century paintings.

A longer way round to Fiesole with a more countrified landscape and still more sights, passes through the village of SETTIGNANO (No. 10 bus from Piazza San Marco), where the baby Michelangelo was put out to nurse—with a stonemason's wife!

Pine liqueur is still distilled in the 13th-century Servite monastery of MONTESENARIO. Breathtaking views over the Arno Valley and surrounding hills from the monastery's terrace.

On the road to SESTO FIORENTINO, visit two grand Medici domiciles, **Villa della Petraia** (closed Mondays) and **Villa di Castello,** with their gardens, fountains and statuary. Just outside Sesto (at Quinto, along the Via Fratelli Rosselli), you'll find a perfectly preserved, remarkably evocative Etruscan tomb, La Montagnola (the Mound).

Another impressive Medici villa is at **Poggio a Caiano** (ring for admittance; closed Mondays). The great hall is richly frescoed with 16th-century allegories especially commemorating Lorenzo the Magnificent who originally bought the place. It's now a pleasant setting for plays and concerts.

Founded in the 14th century and still an active monastery, **Certosa del Galluzzo** (ring for admittance) has some fine frescoes and paintings. Taste or buy the monks' own liqueur, distilled on the spot.

A fine country route leads to a peaceful, centuries' old market town, **Impruneta:** specially interesting in September and October for its famous fairs and various folkloric events. Don't miss the two fine cloisters adjoining the Basilica of Santa Maria dell'Impruneta.

Pisa

The Leaning Tower-cathedral-baptistery trio defies description. The **Piazza del Duomo,** also appropriately known as the Piazza dei Miracoli (the Square of Miracles) is a miracle of human achievement. The **Duomo** was begun around 1063 and finished by 1118 (its fine bronze doors are also 12th century); the **Battistero** took from the 12th to 14th centuries to complete (its acoustics are superb); and the world-famous **bell-tower** with an accidental lean, as beautiful and delicate as carved ivory, was built during the same period (temporarily closed). According to the experts the tower isn't **75**

Pisa's tower permitted Galileo to test the principles of gravity.

cloister-like cemetery whose entire walls are covered with remarkable 14th–15th-century frescoes, some by Benozzo Gozzoli.

It's hard to believe today, but Pisa was once the River Arno's estuary (now at Marina di Pisa, 6½ miles away). A flourishing sea-port colonized by the Greeks, settled by the Etruscans, then the Romans, it had become a rich, powerful naval republic by the 12th century, boasting one of Italy's earliest universities. Long desired and fought over as an outlet to the sea by envious Florence, the city was forcibly grabbed in 1406. Yet only 15 years later its harbour lay silted-up and useless!

Pisa is well worth exploring for its numerous fine churches, palaces, picturesque streets and Museo Nazionale di San Matteo (on Lungarno Mediceo).

You can reach Pisa by train or on a half-day conducted tour. If you have time, visit the historic city of **Pistoia,** with its harmonious Piazza del Duomo, the remarkable silver altar of San Iacopo in the cathedral and its elegant, octagonal baptistery. In **Prato,** known for its beautiful cathedral, see the exterior pulpit by Donatello and Michelozzo and the choir frescoes by Filippo Lippi.

due to fall for quite a few years, but you'll have to adapt to the slight change in angle!

Behind these mighty monuments lies the walled-in **Campo-santo,** a unique 13th-century

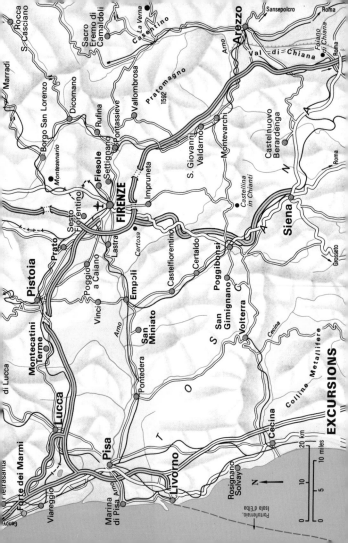

Siena and San Gimignano

Not to be missed for their incomparable medieval atmosphere, you could spend an entire holiday exploring these two cities and the region.

As you approach **Siena** along a road cut through a succession of undulating ruddy-brown hills, you'll understand how the colour "burnt sienna" got its name. The city itself, contrasting with Florence's browns and greys, is a wonderful marriage of brick and stone—all rich reds and warm pinks.

Imposing Gothic architecture prevails everywhere, from the early 14th-century Palazzo Pubblico and its graceful, slender Torre del Mangia, to the cathedral and the many fine *palazzi*.

The huge, sloping, shell-shaped **Piazza del Campo,** where the exciting Palio horse-race takes place every summer, has all the aristocratic grandeur of the Ghibelline city that Siena was—and secretly still is. Traditionally founded by the family of Remus (whose twin Romulus founded Rome), proudest, most stubbornly independent of Tuscan cities, it only fell under Florentine sway in 1555.

In the **Palazzo Pubblico** see Simone Martini's giant frescoes, the *Maestà* (1315)* and the *Condottiere Guidoriccio da Fogliano* on his richly caparisoned horse (1328); note also Ambrogio Lorenzetti's impressive fresco cycle *Good and Bad Government* (1339), the largest painting of the Middle Ages on a non-religious theme.

---

*Authenticity recently disputed.

Walk through picturesquely winding streets to the great Gothic **cathedral** with its striking black-and-white horizontally striped exterior—an echo of the city's arms. See its expanse of inlaid marble floor, its splendid sculptured pulpit and Pinturicchio's colourful historical frescoes in the adjoining Piccolomini Library. And, by all means, don't overlook the **cathedral museum** with Duccio's splendid *Maestà* (1308).

Continue on past the house where, in the 14th century, the city's patroness, St. Catharine of Siena, was born, to the Basilica of San Domenico where her head is preserved. And, still further, visit the impressive church of San Francesco with its Lorenzetti frescoes and the oratory dedicated to another city patron, San Bernardino.

Siena's richly decorated, marble-covered cathedral dominates town.

Renowned for its university (13th century) and its Chigi International Music Academy (concerts from July to September), Siena is also a major linguistics centre—appropriately perhaps, since the purest Italian is said to be spoken here.

It's worth going out of your way to see the **Palio,** a horse race run round the piazza in July and August (see p. 88). Try to reserve a seat in a stand or a place on a balcony, as the crush and excitement down on the *campo* can be harrowing. After a colourful, stately procession of pages, men-at-arms, knights and flag-tossers of the city wards *(contrade)* in the most convincing 15th-century costumes you're ever likely to see, 10 fiercely competing bareback riders race round the piazza for the coveted Palio—a painted silken standard. As you watch this violent spectacle, you'll feel you are taking a step back into the Renaissance.

The nearby 13th-century Palazzo Tolomei (Via Banchi di Sopra) is a magnificent example of private medieval architecture.

Siena also boasts an important art gallery, the **Pinacoteca** (housed in the Palazzo Buonsignori), exhibiting the finest artists of the Siennese school, and an interesting Archives Museum (Palazzo Piccolomini). But don't neglect some souvenir shopping or that famous *panforte* (see p. 84).

The walled medieval town of **San Gimignano** is one of the most evocative and picturesque in Italy. Strategically perched on a hill, it looks even higher because of its 15 stone towers. At one time there were 72 of them. It was a matter of prestige to build the tallest tower possible. The town fell under

Florentine sway in the 14th century.

Stroll through streets and squares little changed since Dante himself came here as a Florentine envoy in 1300. See the 12th-century **Collegiata** church, filled with impressive frescoes, including a fearsome 14th-century *Last Judgement* and the *Martyrdom of St. Sebastian* by Benozzo Gozzoli. Don't miss the chapel of Santa Fina decorated with Ghirlandaio's over-elegant frescoes. Only 15 when she died, this 13th-century mystic was adopted as one of the town's patron saints.

Be sure to visit the 13th–14th-century **Palazzo del Popolo,** with its 177-foot-high tower, its superb little courtyard and unusual frescoes of hunting and courtly love scenes.

Walk up to the **Rocca** or citadel and you'll enjoy a splendid panorama over the town and the valley below. In the 13th-century church of Sant'Agostino, see the fresco in the choir by Benozzo Gozzoli of *Scenes from the Life of St. Augustine,* full of everyday details.

See San Gimignano: living, 14th-century town preserved intact.

What to Do

Shopping

Shopping attractions compete with the sights for tourists' attention—and deserve all the attention they get. Window-shopping is a pleasure in itself. Fashion boutiques catch the eye along smart, expensive Via de' Tornabuoni and Via de' Calzaiuoli; jewellery, silverware, chinaware and leather shops outdo each other in lavish and original displays; colourful merchandise is stacked ten feet high on souvenir market stalls. And almost anywhere you shop, English is understood.

Shops and department stores are open from 8.30 or 9 a.m. until 1 p.m., and from 4 until 8 p.m. From June 15 to September 15 all shops close on Saturday afternoons (on Monday morning the rest of the year). Hairdressers close year-round on Mondays; food shops on Wednesdays.

Best Buys

Fashion. Florentine designers share the limelight with Paris, Rome and London. Exclusive dress or coat models are pricey but still far cheaper than they would be at home. There's always a marvellous selection of smaller designer items like blouses, scarves and belts.

Leather. Part of the fashion scene, you'll see it everywhere. Its tell-tale smell around San Lorenzo and especially Santa Croce will lead you to leather factories where you're shown anything from handbags to wallets and bookmarks being made or finished. There's no obligation to buy.

Don't miss the leather school tucked away behind Santa Croce's sacristy in former Franciscan monk's cells. See apprentices from all over the world cutting, tooling, stamp-

Basketfuls of choices await the shopper in Florence straw-market.

ing traditional motifs. A tempting selection of their work is on sale.

The best buys are gloves, belts, purses, wallets and boxes of all shapes and sizes. Handbags are tempting but almost always expensive, shop and market prices varying little here. As a free bonus you can usually have your initials stamped in gold on any purchase.

Gold and silver. Creative gold jewellery is expensive, but simpler items like gold or silver charms are quite reasonable. You'll want to window-shop along the Ponte Vecchio with its centuries'-old jewellery boutiques, each window more tempting than the last. You won't fail to be impressed by what Florentine designers and craftsmen still produce.

The work of Florentine silversmiths, sometimes inspired by ancient motifs, is invariably beautiful and practical. Look for pill-boxes, napkin rings, photo frames, cruet sets, sugar bowls and candlesticks.

Ceramics and glassware. High quality but expensive table china, ceramic ornaments and innumerable statuettes exist for every taste, largely produced at nearby Sesto Fiorentino. Attractive functional glassware, often very cheap, comes from Empoli or Pisa.

Inlays and mosaics. A Florentine speciality, the art of wood inlay or *intarsio* reached sublime heights in the Renaissance. By the late 16th century, semi-precious stones were often used in inlays; the craft still flourishes. You'll see impressive modern examples for sale in Lungarno Torrigiani, Via Guicciardini and Piazza Santa Croce. Larger items like tables are inevitably expensive; small, naïve, framed "pictures" of birds, flowers, Tuscan landscapes or views of Florence are charming curiosities and comparatively cheap.

If budding Cellinis are hard to find in Florence today, skilful artisans are not: those colourful, delicate glass mosaic brooches, pendants, bracelets and rings you see everywhere are made at home by armies of patient Florentine women. With no two items identical, they're unquestionably the cheapest, best value-for-money trinkets.

To eat and drink. The sweet-toothed should take or send home succulent Italian candied chestnuts; a selection of nutty *torrone* (nougat); delicious ready-boxed biscuits from Siena or the famous Sienese *panforte,* a rich, chewy mixture

of nuts and spiced candied fruits. And don't leave without one of those quaint aromatic monastery liqueurs or a genuine *fiasco* of Chianti to help you remember it all by.

Antiques and Repros

Antiques have been prized in Florence for over five centuries: a major international antique fair is now held biennially at the Palazzo Strozzi (September–October).

Antique shops cluster mainly around Borgo Ognissanti and San Jacopo, Via della Vigna Nuova and della Spada. Specializing largely in furniture, paintings and decorations,

none of them are cheap. Bric-à-brac and knicknacks are virtually non-existent.

Flea-market addicts will find a permanent, modest-sized one on Piazza dei Ciompi (open daily in full season).

If you can't afford an old master, treat yourself to a good reproduction, a Florentine speciality. You can get a full-size version of your favourite statue or any piece of "antique" furniture made to order.

Framed reproduction 18th-century prints of Florence are good buys, especially around Piazza del Duomo. Look for unframed prints in San Lorenzo market. Or try one of **85** those little men in the Uffizi busily putting finishing touches to oil copies of Raphaels and Caravaggios. Arms and armour fans can consider inexpensive suits of armour, swords, pistols and conquistador helmets near the Bargello.

Markets

Obvious answers for tourists in a hurry, they're part of the local colour. Conveniently central is the Mercato Nuovo, or Straw Market. Under its loggia (built in 1547), a score of stalls offer masses of attractive straw-work bags, sunhats, semi-precious stone trinkets, glass-mosaic jewellery, reproduction Davids, typical Florentine gilt-patterned wooden articles and so on.

San Lorenzo market caters for tourists and locals selling everything from tools to crocodile handbags. Stretching around Piazza San Lorenzo, its crowded, tempting food-shops add to the bustle and atmosphere. There's clothing, shoes and leatherware here, often at bargain prices. Several stalls even accept credit cards; many take travellers' cheques and will send purchases anywhere.

Haggling, once a tourist must, is fast dying out. With prices more strictly controlled,

there's little need for it, unless buying several items. Shops and boutiques frown on it and often post categorical *prezzi fissi* (fixed prices) notices. At most suggest a "rounding-off" of your bill or expect a small free knicknack if making a sizeable purchase.

Nightlife

Florence boasts many discotheques and dance halls, a few night-clubs, plus some open-air dancing establishments in the summer around the Viale Michelangelo and Fiesole. Hotel receptionists or tourist offices will supply addresses.

After a torrid summer's day spent playing hide-and-seek with the sun, Florentines make the most of the only slightly cooler evenings and take to the streets. Entire family clans, from toddlers to grannies, stroll round the centre, window-shop, sit gossiping in doorways or at crowded open-air café tables, a good-natured, leisurely throng.

Join them. Eat a *gelato,* a slice of piping-hot pizza or cool watermelon, or sit at a café and listen to the babel of voices—foreign and Italian—all around you. Try the cafés on Piazza della Repubblica. One of them offers a regular song-and-band show loud enough to entertain not only its customers but the entire piazza.

If you've a car, drive a few miles out of Florence to discover quaint, unsophisticated country restaurants. One good place to try is Pontassieve (18 km from Florence). Or just take a bus up to Piazzale Michelangelo and see the city by night. You'll never be at a loss for something relaxing to do in the evening.

Events and Festivals

Whatever the time of year, there's bound to be something interesting going on in Florence, whether it's a special art, antique, or handicraft exhibition at the Palazzo Strozzi, a dog or fashion show, a flower show (May and October) or a bit of historic folklore. It's worth obtaining the handy month-by-month *Calendar of Events in Florence and its Province* from the tourist office.

Concerts are a year-round feature: in July and August, open-air evening concerts are given in the Boboli Gardens; organ recitals in historic churches in September and October. During June, July and August nearby Fiesole offers a festival of concerts, ballet, drama and films—much of it in its Roman theatre. In June and September, the beautiful Medici villa at Poggio a Caiano serves as the setting for plays and concerts. The Florentine opera season is December to February and July.

But if you can, plan to attend the celebrated Maggio Musicale Fiorentino festival (mid-May to end of June) which attracts some of the finest concert, ballet and operatic performers in the world. **87**

Annual events in and around Florence

Annunciation Day (March): City celebrations.

Easter Sunday: *Scoppio del Carro.* Noonday fireworks in Piazza del Duomo.

Ascension Day (May): *Festa del Grillo.* Crickets in tiny cages sold at the Cascine to be set free.

St. John's Day (June 24 and 28): *Giuoco del Calcio.* Traditional rough, tough football game in 16th-century costume. Fireworks in Piazzale Michelangelo.

July 2 and August 16: *Palio di Siena.* Historic pageant and horse race in Siena's main square.

September 7: *Festa delle Rificolone.* Impressive bridge (Ponte San Niccolò) and river evening procession with torches and paper lanterns.

September: Bird Fair at Porta Romana.

See also PUBLIC HOLIDAYS in the Blueprint section of this book.

Sports

Swimming. If walking around Florence isn't enough, you'll certainly find other outlets for your energies. Swim or just sunbathe at the modern Piscina Bellariva (Lungarno Colombo), or Rari Nantes (Lungarno Ferrucci) or Piscina Costoli (Campo di Marte) which offer attractive children's facilities. Or try the more sophisticated, club-like pool at the Cascine. A cross between London's Hyde Park and New York's Central Park in miniature, even boasting a tiny zoo, the Cascine (the name means "dairies") are pleasant to stroll in—but better avoided after dark.

To enjoy a dip in the sea, you have to travel to Viareggio, Forte dei Marmi, Marina di Pisa or Tirrenia.

Tennis. Would-be tennis players won't get a look-in at the exclusive Cascine tennis club. But there are courts in the Viale Michelangelo, as well as a golf-tennis-swimming complex, the Campi dell'Ugolino, just south of Florence. The tourist office (see p.122), which owns this last establishment, will supply all relevant information.

Riding. Riding facilities are skimpy: you have to go to Impruneta (14 km away). But you can watch trotting or flat racing at the Cascine.

Walking. There are endless possibilities for fascinating walks, hikes or drives that take you right out into those green, undulating hills all around, and to closer places like Bellosguardo park, Piazzale Michelangelo, Certosa del Galluzzo monastery, Poggio Imperiale or the Arcetri observatory—that stands on the very hill from which Galileo gazed at the stars. The tourist office supplies a useful map of Florence province and will advise on routes to take.

Wining and Dining

If measure and simplicity are the keynotes of Tuscan architecture, you could say the same of its cuisine.* Tuscans, and Florentines most of all, have always verged on the fanatical about fresh "country" fare. Fiercely proud of their olive oil, their bread, their wine, they're more likely to wax lyrical over a plateful of tender boiled marrows *(zucchini),* a *pecorino* cheese or some freshly picked local figs, than over an elaborate dish. Plain-minded or not, well-to-do Florentines of the 16th century commonly ate with knives and forks—perhaps designed by Cellini—while the rest of Europe was still happily using its fingers.

Fussy, yet notoriously unadventurous with exotic or foreign foods, the nearest they get to "disguising" the natural flavour of anything is a fairly generous use of olive oil, sage, rosemary, basil and, of course, tomato in many of their dishes. But you have to admit the raw materials here are superb. Take a morning stroll through the busy markets around San Lorenzo and on Piazza Santo Spirito. See and smell the exhilarating freshness of everything, and you'll be convinced. Meat and poultry in Florence are among the best you'll taste in Italy, but sea-food and fish are likely to be expensive. In season, fresh game (boar, hare, partridge, pheasant, deer) appears on Florentine tables.

From Maestros to Mammas

Restaurants range from expensive establishments to modest family *trattorie.* All restaurants must issue a formal receipt indicating the sales tax or VAT *(I.V.A.).* A customer may be stopped outside the premises and fined if unable to produce a receipt. The bill usually includes cover *(coperto)* and service *(servizio)* charges as well. Leave about 10 per cent for the waiter.

All but the cheaper *trattorie* offer a "safe" but unimaginative three-course, fixed-price *menu turistico.* Students with international cards can get special discounts in some restaurants—ask the waiter about the cheaper rates. But today's cost-conscious tourists and Florentines are generously catered for by hordes of little sandwich, pizza and coffee bars.

You'll find, too, some coun-

*For a comprehensive glossary of Italian wining and dining, ask your bookshop for the Berlitz EUROPEAN MENU READER.

ter-service *tavola calda* establishments, and a handful of pleasant, family-run self-service restaurants offering good cheap food.

If it's atmosphere and Tuscan accents you're after, try the streets around the Ponte Vecchio, Santo Spirito, Santa Croce and San Lorenzo. And if you're feeling fairly adventurous, try a slab of scalding fried *polenta* (purée of maize, or cornmeal), a *crostino* (chopped chicken liver on fried bread) or at least a *bombolone* (doughnut) at a *friggitoría* (fry-shop).

First Courses

Among the usual all-Italian starters, look out for local specialities like *prosciutto crudo con fichi* (raw ham with fresh figs), *crostini, fettunta* (toasted country bread rubbed with garlic and sprinkled with olive oil), *minestra di fagioli* (thick butter-bean soup), *minestrone* (even thicker vegetable soup) **91** and *ribollita* (a bread-based vegetable soup), served hot or cold in summer.

Among the 360 known varieties of Italian pasta, try *pappardelle* (broad noodles, served in season with hare sauce), *paglia e fieno* ("straw and hay"— mixed white and green pasta), *ravioli con panna* (ravioli in fresh cream sauce), as well as the ever-popular *lasagne* or *tortellini*. Remember you can always order a half portion *(mezza porzione)* of pasta.

Meat and Fish
The famous *bistecca alla fiorentina,* a mammoth charcoal-grilled T-bone steak, served with lemon, is a must at least once. It's always expensive: make sure that they show you your meat first and tell you its weight (the price per kilo is normally marked on the menu). It's quite in order for two people to share one *bistecca*: Florentines do it all the time. Try also *arista* (roast loin of pork), *bollito di manzo* or just *lesso* (boiled beef served with a piquant sauce), *trippe alla fiorentina* (tripe cooked with ham, tomato and parmesan), *fritto misto* (deep-fried mixed meats and vegetables) and all kinds of liver *alla fiorentina,* sautéed and flavoured with sage or rosemary.

Chicken *(pollo)* crops up regularly in Tuscan cooking, and you'll probably taste it either *alla cacciatora* (with tomatoes and vegetables), *alla diavola* (charcoal-grilled), *arrosto* (roast) or as *petti di pollo saltati* or *fritti* (chicken breasts sautéed or fried). Hare and rabbit frequently appear *alla cacciatora.*

There's less emphasis on fish dishes in Florentine menus, but two you're almost certain to find are *baccalà alla fiorentina* (a robust cod stew) and the highly tasty Livornese *cacciucco* (red mullet or other fish cooked in tomatoes, onion, garlic and red wine, served on garlic-flavoured croutons).

Vegetables

In Italy vegetables *(contorno)* are usually served and charged for apart. Sample *carciofini fritti* (crisply fried artichokes), *frittata di carciofi* (artichoke omelette) or, in autumn, a plateful of grilled mushrooms *(funghi).* Try also *fagiolini* or *fagioli all'uccelletto* (boiled green or butter-beans sautéed with tomato and sage), *al fiasco* (same ingredients, baked) or *alla fiorentina* (boiled, simply seasoned with oil, salt and pepper, eaten almost cold) or just settle for an *insalata mista* (mixed salad).

Sweets

For a satisfying dessert, have a slice of *zuccotto,* a large liqueur-soaked, chilled sponge and chocolate cake, a piece of *torta* (cake or tart), or just *frutta di stagione* (fresh fruit). But for a really delightful treat on a warm summer's evening, you can't improve on a cool, juicy slice of watermelon *(anguria* or *cocomero)* bought at one of those colourful street stalls dotted about the city. Ice cream is also a must in Florence (see p. 94).

Doing It Yourself

If you fancy a change from *trattorie* and sandwich bars, take a picnic among the statues in the Loggia dei Lanzi, in the Boboli Gardens, in Fiesole or up on the terrace of San Miniato with all Florence at your feet. Buy fresh fruit and bread, then make for any one of the hundreds of delicatessens *(pizzicheria).* Crammed with mouthwatering merchandise from floor to ceiling, fun just to browse through, they stock virtually anything edible and drinkable, including wine and soft drinks, and often sell sandwich rolls *(panino ripieno).* They'll usually oblige by filling your own rolls with whatever you buy, saving you time and mess.

Occasional picnics are the best way to sample specialities you won't find so easily elsewhere. Try *finocchiona*, Tuscany's own garlic- and fennel-flavoured salami, and don't neglect the whole rich Italian range of cured hams, salamis, *mortadella* sausage, etc. As for cheeses, taste *ricotta* (creamy cottage cheese), *stracchino*, *pecorino* (a tangy ewe's-milk cheese), *caciotta*, *provola* (smoked or fresh) and, of course, *gorgonzola, parmigiano* or *grana*—the younger variety you eat rather than grate. Delicious with fresh bread and fruit! But don't forget: all food shops are closed on Wednesday afternoons.

Beating the Heat

If the city's summer heat deadens your appetite, you can always fall back on drinks. If Florence as a whole suffers from a shortage of spacious open air cafés to sit and relax in, fashionable ones in the Piazza della Signoria and Piazza della Repubblica are *the* places for aperitifs, appointments, postcard-writing or afternoon tea, while the Via de' Tornabuoni has its share of chic, busy tea-rooms.

In any case, you'll never be at a loss for thirst-quenchers anywhere in Florence—from

good Italian beers *(birra)* aperitifs and cocktails, to iced tamarind juice *(tamarindo)* non-alcoholic bitters, fresh fruit juice *(spremuta)*, fruit shake *(frullato)*, and coffee or lemon poured over crushed ice *(granita)*. For children there's always fizzy orange or lemonade *(aranciata* or *limonata)* and, naturally, a bewildering choice of succulent ice-creams *(gelato)*. For really off-beat flavours (like fig, chestnut or peach) try the Piazza delle

Cure, Via de' Calzaiuoli, the Ponte Vecchio area or Piazza San Simone.

Wines and Spirits

To a lot of people outside Italy Chianti *is* Italian wine—small wonder, perhaps, since Englishmen were already drinking it at home in the late 17th century. Tuscany's number one wine, it's produced around Florence, Pistoia, Pisa, Siena and Arezzo.

Those picturesque but practical straw-covered *fiaschi*—the most famous wine bottles in the world—conjure up instant visions of Sunny Italy. With rising costs, this bit of real folklore is sadly giving way to ugly plastic imitations. So hoard your *fiasco* for posterity.

Compile your own menu from copious choice at an Italian pizzicheria.

A red, light wine, Chianti can be drunk with almost anything. Quality and price can vary, but it's generally very acceptable and occasionally superlative. If you're bent on trying a really fine Chianti *(Chianti Classico)* straight from Tuscany's top vineyards, make sure the neck of your bottle bears a seal with a black cock on it. Bottles with a cherub on the seal also guarantee absolute authenticity and high quality.

If you've a passion for wine, choose one of several organized coach trips to the finest Chianti cellars with their mighty oak casks and millions of bottles. You'll be taking in some superb sights and countryside at the same time (July to October; details are available from the tourist office; see p. 122). You can buy wines you've tasted on the spot, often at extremely low prices.

The Chianti label extends to the similar *Rufina,* and to another more full-bodied red, *Montalbano.* But Chianti is certainly not on its own. There are other light reds, *Montecarlo* and *Brolio; Aleatico di Porto-ferraio* (from Elba); an unusual, slightly bitter red, *Nobile di Montepulciano;* and a fine dry red, *Brunello di Montalcino,* all worth trying.

Among the few Tuscan white wines are the excellent dry *Vernaccia di San Gimignano, Montecarlo* and the mellower *bianco dell'Elba* (the Isle of Elba was for long a Tuscan possession, prized for its wine). From Elba, too, comes a range of white *spumante* (sparkling wine), just the thing to round off a celebration meal.

Don't feel compelled to order wine with every meal, there's always a choice of fizzy and still mineral water, or beer. Florence's tap water is heavily chlorinated, but it's drinkable.

Tuscans often like to end their meal with a small glass of *Vinsanto* ("holy wine"), a deep amber-coloured sweet wine. If you're lucky enough to visit a local farmer or family, you'll almost certainly be welcomed with some *Vinsanto,* whatever the time of day. Most bars and cafés serve it by the glass. Or try it as an aperitif.

You'll also find a dizzying array of aperitifs, digestives, bitters *(amari)* of which Italians are so fond, brandies, foreign spirits (Scotch whisky is amazingly cheap) and intriguing herb liqueurs made by monks in nearby monasteries. The trouble is that you won't have time to sample them all!

To Help You Order...

Good evening. I'd like a table.
Do you have a set menu?

**Buona sera. Vorrei un tavolo.
Avete un menù a prezzo fisso?**

I'd like a/an/some...

Vorrei...

beer	**una birra**	milk	**del latte**
bread	**del pane**	mineral	**dell'acqua**
butter	**del burro**	water	**minerale**
coffee	**un caffè**	napkin	**un tovagliolo**
cream	**della panna**	potatoes	**delle patate**
dessert	**un dolce**	salad	**dell'insalata**
fish	**del pesce**	soup	**una minestra**
fruit	**della frutta**	spoon	**un cucchiaio**
glass	**un bicchiere**	sugar	**dello zucchero**
ice-cream	**un gelato**	tea	**un tè**
meat	**della carne**	wine	**del vino**

...and Read the Menu

aglio	garlic	**maiale**	pork
agnello	lamb	**manzo**	beef
anitra	duck	**melanzana**	aubergine
antipasto	hors d'œuvre		(eggplant)
arrosto	roast	**peperoni**	peppers
baccalà	dried cod	**pesce**	fish
bistecca	steak	**pollo**	chicken
braciola	chop	**prosciutto**	ham
calamari	squid	**crudo**	cured
carciofi	artichokes	**cotto**	cooked
cipolle	onions	**risotto**	rice dish
coniglio	rabbit	**rognoni**	kidneys
fagioli	beans	**salsa**	sauce
fegato	liver	**sogliola**	sole
formaggio	cheese	**spinaci**	spinachs
fragole	strawberries	**stufato**	stew
frittata	omelette	**triglia**	red mullet
frutti di	seafood	**trippe**	tripe
mare		**uova**	eggs
funghi	mushrooms	**vitello**	veal
gamberi	prawns	**zuppa**	soup

97

BLUEPRINT for a Perfect Trip

How to Get There

BY AIR

Scheduled flights

Florence's airport, Peretola, has regular connections with all major airports in Italy. It now also has international flights to and from Brussels, Monaco, Nice, Olbia, Paris, Vienna and Lugano. The larges

international airport close to Florence is Pisa. However, Rome and Milan are the main gateways to Italy, both for international and inter-continental flights. From Rome or Milan you can transfer to a flight to Pisa, continuing by train from Pisa Airport to Florence, or take a direct flight from Milan or Rome to Florence's airport.

Charter flights and package tours

If you decide on a package tour or charter, read your contract care-fully before you sign. Most tour agents recommend cancellation insurance, a modestly priced safeguard.

From the U.K. and Ireland: Package tours featuring Florence are numerous, ranging from stays of four to 14 nights. It is worth noting that most package tours are on a room-only or just Continental-break-fast basis. A few provide a half-board arrangement but at a supple-ment. Flights are out of Gatwick or Heathrow, and the prime Italian operator also offers a rail-package deal departing from London Vic-toria. Florence is heavily featured in two-centre stays in conjunction with Rome and the Tuscan resorts and hills or with the Italian Lakes, although the rail package is not always available for such tours.

From North America: Package deals including hotel, car or other land arrangements can be very good value. In addition to APEX and Ex-cursion fares, there's the Advance Booking Charter (ABC), usually also for flight only, which must be bought at least 30 days in advance.

BY CAR

The main access roads to Florence are: from France via Lyons to Turin, then by A21 and A26 to Genoa and A12 to Pisa, or via the French Riviera through Genoa; from Switzerland via the Grand St. Bernard Pass and by the A5 and A26 to Genoa, or via the Simplon or Gotthard passes to Milan and by A1 through Bologna; from Austria via the Brenner Pass and A22 (E6) through Modena.

BY RAIL

From London or Paris, the Rome Express takes you to Pisa (where you change for Florence) via Turin and Genoa.

Inter-Rail and Rail Europ Senior cards: The Inter-Rail Card permits 30 days of unlimited rail travel in participating European countries to people under 26. The Rail Europ Senior Card is available for senic citizens and entitles the holder to a discount on European and interna Italian rail journeys.

Eurailpass and Eurail Youthpass: Non-European residents ca travel on these flat-rate, unlimited mileage tickets valid for rail trav anywhere in Western Europe outside of Great Britain. You must bu your pass before leaving home.

The Italian State Railways offer fare reductions in certain cases, pa ticularly for large families. The BTLC Tourist Ticket *(Biglietto Turis tico di Libera Circolazione)* is valid for specified periods of unlimite travel within Italy in either first of second class. Inquire, too, abou the advantageous Kilometric Ticket *(Biglietto Chilometrico),* whic may be used by up to 5 people. These tickets can be purchased at hom or in Italy.

When to Go

Despite its central position on the Italian peninsula, Florence is one o the country's hottest cities in summer. The worst period is mid-June t mid-September, but in early spring and late autumn the weather i more variable.

It's best to visit Florence in April and May, or September and October, when the city is less crowded. During the fashion show (October and March/April) hotels tend to be overbooked, so try to arrange your holidays outside those weeks. Easter time is also ver busy, so it's best to reserve far ahead for travel and hotels. It's als wise to check with your travel agency about the dates of the variou fashion shows in Florence at the Fortezza da Basso, during whic most hotels are fully booked.

Air temperature		J	F	M	A	M	J	J	A	S	O	N	I
Max.	F	48	53	59	68	75	84	89	88	82	70	57	5(
	C	9	12	16	20	24	29	32	31	28	21	14	1(
Min.	F	35	36	40	46	53	59	62	61	59	52	43	3
	C	2	2	5	8	12	15	17	17	15	11	6	

Figures shown are approximate monthly averages

Planning Your Budget

To give you an idea of what to expect, here are some average prices in Italian lire (L.). However, inflation makes them unavoidably approximate, and there are considerable seasonal differences.

Airport transfer. Train from Pisa airport to Florence L. 5,700.

Baby-sitters. L. 15,000–18,000 per hour.

Bus service. Flat-rate fare for Florence and suburbs L. 800.

Camping (high season). Adults L. 7,150 per person per night, children L. 4,200, camper or caravan (trailer) L. 8,500, car and tent L. 12,200, motorbike L. 2,200.

Car hire (international company). *Fiat Uno* L. 100,000 per day, L. 580,000 per week with unlimited mileage. *Fiat Tipo* or *Alfa 33* L. 115,000 per day, L. 650,000 per week with unlimited mileage. *Alfa 75* L. 150,000 per day, L. 820,000 per week with unlimited mileage. Tax is included.

Cigarettes (packet of 20). Italian brands L. 2,200 and up, imported brands L. 3,350 and up.

Entertainment. Cinema L. 10,000, discotheque (entry and one drink) L. 35,000.

Hairdressers. *Woman's* shampoo and set or blow-dry L. 25,000–35,000, permanent wave L. 55,000–80,000. *Man's* haircut L. 17,000, with shampoo L. 25,000.

Hotels (double room with bath, including tax and services). ***** L. 450,000–600,000, **** L. 300,000–400,000, *** L. 100,000–200,000, ** L. 70,000–100,000, * L. 50,000–70,000.

Meals and drinks. Continental breakfast L. 10,000–25,000, lunch/dinner in fairly good establishment L. 35,000–84,000, coffee served at a table L. 2,500–5,000, served at the bar L. 1,100–2,200, bottle of wine L. 7,500 and up, soft drink L. 2,000 and up, aperitif L. 2,500 and up.

Museums. L. 8,000.

Shopping bag. 500 g. of bread L. 1,225, 250 g. of butter L. 2,480 and up, 6 eggs L. 1,590, 500 g. of beefsteak L. 8,950–12,000, 250 g. of coffee L. 3,430, bottle of wine L. 4,000 and up.

Youth hostels. L. 16,400 per night with breakfast.

An A–Z Summary of
Practical Information and Facts

> Listed after most entries is the appropriate Italian translation, usually in the singular, plus a number of phrases that may come in handy during your stay in Italy.

A **ACCOMMODATION** (see also CAMPING). Florence's tourist office publishes an annual list of hotels *(albergo)*, boarding-houses *(pensione)* and inns *(locanda)* for the city and its immediate environs. It supplies full details on amenities, prices and classification (1 to 5 stars). You can obtain it in the Florence tourist office or from the Italian State Tourist Office (E.N.I.T.) in your country.

During spring, summer and early autumn it's always advisable to book ahead, but for the rest of the year you'll have no problem finding accommodation, except during trade fairs. In Florence, hotel reservations can be made at the I.T.A. *(Informazioni Turistiche Alberghiere)* counter at the railway station (normally from 9 a.m. to 8.30 p.m. daily).

On page 101 you'll find some average rates for a double room in summer season. Off-season rates are somewhat lower. Single rooms cost 60 to 70% the price of doubles. Breakfast, which you're expected to take at the hotel, is not included in the room rate. Unless prices are noted as *tutto compreso* (all inclusive), as much as 20% in tax and service can be added to the bill. A few major hotels have swimming pools, and some hotels on the outskirts have tennis courts.

Youth Hostels *(ostello della gioventù)*. If you're planning to make extensive use of youth hostels during your stay in Italy, contact your national youth hostel association before departure to obtain an international membership card. The Florence branch of the Associazione Italiana Alberghi per la Gioventù is at:

Viale Augusto Righi, 2; tel. 60 03 15

In full season (especially July) certain religious institutions such as convents or monasteries open their doors to young people. Check with the tourist office.

Day hotels. Florence has two *alberghi diurni*—"day-time hotels"—one in the main railway station, Stazione Centrale (F.S.), where you can hire a room for a few hours' rest. It also provides bathrooms, hairdressers, laundry facilities, etc. (open from 6 a.m. to about 8 p.m. with early closing on Sundays).

I'd like a single/double room.	**Vorrei una camera singola/ matrimoniale.**
with bath/shower	**con bagno/doccia**
What's the rate per night?	**Qual è il prezzo per una notte?**

AIRPORT *(aeroporto)*. Florence's small international airport, Peretola, which also serves all the major Italian cities, does not have many flights per day and is, therefore, heavily booked far ahead.

The largest airport closest to Florence is Pisa's Galileo Galilei (San Giusto). From the Pisa airport there is an hourly train service to Florence which takes about an hour. Otherwise, you can hire a car at the Pisa airport and get to Florence, also in about an hour.

Take these bags to the bus/train/taxi, please.	**Mi porti queste valige fino all'autobus/al treno/al taxi, per favore.**
What time does the train for Florence leave?	**A che ora parte il treno per Firenze?**

CAMPING *(campeggio)*. Six major camping sites are located in the immediate vicinity of Florence, two within easy reach of the centre by bus. For information on facilities in and around Florence, contact the tourist office (see p. 122).

In Italy, you may camp freely outside of sites if you obtain permission either from the owner of the property or from the local authorities. For your personal safety you should choose sites where there are other campers.

If you enter Italy with a caravan (trailer) you must be able to show an inventory (with two copies) of the material and equipment in the caravan: dishes, linen, etc.

May we camp here?	**Possiamo campeggiare qui?**
Is there a campsite near here?	**C'è un campeggio qui vicino?**
We have a tent/caravan (trailer).	**Abbiamo la tenda/la roulotte.**

CAR HIRE *(autonoleggio)* (see also DRIVING). Your hotel or the yellow pages of the telephone book will supply the addresses of the leading hire firms. Depending on the location of your hotel, you can ask for a hire car to be delivered there. However, since the major car-hire firms are located near the railway station, it is easier to walk over and pick it up. If you have heavy luggage, take a taxi from the station to your hotel, then pick up your car or have it delivered. Delivery at the railway station is not possible, because a new underground parking garage is being constructed—there is neither parking nor stopping.

Firms usually offer a range of Fiats; other Italian and foreign models are less frequently available. Minimum age varies from 18 to 25 according to company. Insurance is mandatory. Normally a deposit is charged when hiring a car, but holders of major credit cards are exempt. Special weekend rates and weekly unlimited mileage rates for foreigners may be available. Inquire, too, about any available seasonal deals.

I'd like to rent a car.	**Vorrei noleggiare una macchina.**

CIGARETTES, CIGARS, TOBACCO *(sigarette, sigari, tabacco)*. The cheapest Italian cigarettes are considered somewhat rough by many foreigners. Most foreign brands are on sale in any tobacco shop *(tabaccheria)* in a hotel district. Foreign menthol cigarettes are also available. Officially, tobacco and matches may be sold only in shops bearing a large sign with a white *T* on a dark background which is mounted over the entrance—or at certain authorized hotel news-stands and café counters.

Ask for a *toscano* and you'll get a very pungent black cigar that's been smoked in Florence for generations. It's better to smell than to smoke, but it's part of the local colour.

I'd like a packet of...	**Vorrei un pacchetto di...**
with/without filter	**con/senza filtro**
I'd like a box of matches, please.	**Per favore, mi dia una scatola di fiammiferi.**

CLOTHING. At least from May to September you'll wear summer-weight clothes in Florence; women will find a light wrap useful occa-sionally in the evening. A wrap is also handy to cover bare shoulders when visiting churches.

Slacks for women are acceptable everywhere. But miniskirts, shorts and bare-backed dresses are frowned upon in churches. The tradi-tional custom that a woman should cover her head with a scarf or hat in church is giving way to a bare-headed new generation, and most priests don't seem to mind.

COMMUNICATIONS

Post offices *(ufficio postale)* handle telegrams, mail and money transfers, and some have public telephones. Stamps are also sold at tobacconists *(tabaccheria)* and at some hotel desks. Florentine post boxes are red. The slot marked *Per la città* is for local mail only; *Altre destinazioni* for mail going elsewhere.

Post office **hours** are normally from 8.15 a.m. to 1.40 p.m., Monday to Friday, until 12 noon on Saturdays.

The conveniently located post office in Via Maso Finiguerra is open for all services from 8 a.m. to 6.30 p.m. (including lunchtime). Other main branches, such as those at Via Pellicceria (off Piazza della Repubblica) and Viale Belfiore, function until 7 p.m. but only for registered mail and other special services. Via Pellicceria has 24-hour telephone and telegram facilities; use the bell outside the main entrance when the doors are locked.

Poste restante (general delivery). It's not worth arranging to receive mail during a brief visit to Florence as Italy's postal system is rather unreliable. Instead, have people cable or telephone your hotel. If you're going to be in Florence for a considerable time and must have things sent to you, there is poste-restante *(fermo posta)* service at the Via Pellicceria post office (see above). Don't forget your passport as identification when you go to pick up mail. Have mail addressed in this way:

> Mr. John Smith
> Fermo Posta
> Palazzo delle Poste
> Via Pellicceria
> Florence, Italy

Telegrams *(telegramma):* These can be sent to destinations inside and outside Italy, as can telex messages. There is now a rapidly growing **telefax** (facsimile) service.

Parcels *(pacco):* Bureaucratic regulations about wrapping and sending packages from Italy are so complicated that even immensely knowledgeable hotel concierges don't know them all. Ask at a post office.

Telephone *(telefono).* Here's another challenge in Florence. Glass-enclosed booths are scattered throughout the city, and almost every bar and café has a public telephone, indicated by a yellow sign just outside showing a telephone dial. Older types of public payphones require

C tokens *(gettoni;* available from machines [generally installed next to the telephone] and at bars, hotels, post offices and tobacconists'), more modern phones, with three separate slots, take *gettoni,* coins and telephone cards *(scheda telefonica).* Phone cards are available from tobacconists and some news-stands, and cost either L. 5,000 or L. 10,000.

Calls to other Italian cities and abroad can be dialled directly from local phone boxes. International telephone offices are located at Via Cavour, 21 (Centro Telefonici Pubblici SIP), at the post offices in Via Pellicceria and Via Pietrapiana and at the railway station.

To make a call you insert a coin, token or card and lift the receiver. A dial tone is a series of regular dash-dash sounds which you may not hear for several seconds. A dot-dot-dot series means Florence's central computer is overloaded—hang up and try again. Or you may finish dialling and then hear nothing at all. When you absolutely must reach a local number but find it engaged, dial 197, wait for a gong and tape-recorded instructions before continuing, then dial your number. This will ensure a message is sent to the desired number to the effect that there is an urgent call waiting to get through.

Some useful numbers:

Domestic directory inquiries (information):	12
International operator	170
Telegrams	186

Give me ... *gettoni/* a telephone card, please.	**Per favore, mi dia ... gettoni/** **una scheda telefonica.**
Have you received any mail for...?	**C'è posta per ...?**
I'd like a stamp for this letter/ postcard.	**Desidero un francobollo per** **questa lettera/cartolina.**
airmail	**via aerea**
registered	**raccomandata**
I want to send a telegram to...	**Desidero mandare un** **telegramma a ...**

COMPLAINTS *(reclamo).* Complaining is an Italian national pastime, but can involve elaborate bureaucratic procedures once it passes beyond the verbal stage. In hotels, restaurants and shops, complaints should be made to the manager or proprietor.

If satisfaction is not quickly obtained, mention that you intend to **106** report the matter to the tourist office (see TOURIST INFORMATION

OFFICES), or to the regular police (*Questura*, see POLICE). The threat of a formal declaration to the police should be effective in such cases as overcharging for car repairs, but this will consume hours or even days of your visit.

    To avoid problems in all situations, always establish the price in advance—especially when dealing with porters at stations. Any complaint about a taxi fare should be settled by referring to a notice, in four languages, affixed by law in each taxi, specifying extra charges (airport runs, Sunday or holiday rates, night surcharge) in excess of the meter rate.

CONSULATES. Citizens from countries which have no consulate in Florence should get in touch with their embassy in Rome.

Australia: (Rome) Via Alessandria, 215; tel. 83 27 21

Canada: (Rome) Via G. Battista De Rossi, 27; tel. 841 53 41/4

Eire: (Rome) Largo del Nazareno, 3; tel. 678 25 41

United Kingdom: Lungarno Corsini, 2; tel. 28 41 33

U.S.A.: Lungarno A. Vespucci, 38; tel. 29 82 76/21 76 05

South Africa: (Rome) Via Tanaro 14–16; tel. 844 97 94

Where is the British/American consulate?

Dov'è il consolato britannico/ americano?

CONVERTER CHARTS. For distance measures, see p. 112. Italy uses the metric system.

Temperature

Length

Weight

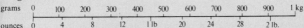

107

C **COURTESIES.** Although less formal than many other Europeans, Italians do appreciate certain social courtesies. Upon entering and leaving a shop, restaurant or office, the expected greeting is always *buon giorno* (good morning) or *buona sera* (good evening) from as early as 1 p.m. onwards. When approaching anyone with an inquiry, start with *per favore* (please), and for any service say *grazie* (thanks), to which the reply is *prego* (don't mention it; you're welcome). Introductions to men, women and older children are always accompanied by a handshake, the proper phrase being *piacere* (it's a pleasure). After you know an Italian well, *ciao* is the common phrase of greeting.

How are you?	**Come sta?**
Very well, thanks.	**Molto bene, grazie.**

CRIME and THEFT. Violent crime is, happily, rare in Florence. Though women may be pestered, such attention is unlikely to escalate beyond acceptable bounds. Pickpockets work feverishly on the bus routes. For this reason, if travelling by bus, women should have purses that can be zipped up—and hold them tight. Men should never leave their wallets in back pockets. It's wise to leave your unneeded documents and excess money in the hotel safe.

Shady characters may offer stolen goods (especially transistors, watches, cameras) or "bargain" items which are likely to be of extremely poor workmanship though apparently brand-new.

Theft of cars or of their contents can best be avoided by emptying them of everything—not only of valuables. Leave the glove compartments empty and open to discourage prospective thieves. If your hotel has a private garage or guarded parking lot, leave your car there.

I want to report a theft.	**Voglio denunciare un furto.**
My wallet/passport/ticket has been stolen.	**Mi hanno rubato il portafoglio/ il passaporto/il biglietto.**

CUSTOMS *(dogana)* **and ENTRY REGULATIONS.** For a stay of up to three months, a valid passport is sufficient for citizens of Australia, Canada, New Zealand and U.S.A. Visitors from Eire and the United Kingdom need only an identity card to enter Italy.

Italian customs officials are unlikely to quibble over smaller points: they are interested mainly in detecting smuggled art treasures, currency or narcotics. If you're exporting archaeological relics, works of art, or gems, you should obtain a bill of sale and a permit from the government (this is normally handled by the dealer).

Here's what you can take into Italy duty-free and, when returning home, into your own country:

Entering Italy from:	Cigarettes		Cigars		Tobacco	Spirits		Wine
1)	200	or	50	or	250 g.	¾ l.	or	2 l.
2)	300	or	75	or	400 g.	1.5 l.	or	3 l.
3)	400	or	100	or	500 g.	¾ l.	or	2 l.
Into:								
Australia	250	or	250 g. or		250 g.	1 l.	or	1 l.
Canada	200	and	50	and	900 g.	1.1 l.	or	1.1 l.
Eire	200	or	50	or	250 g.	1 l.	and	2 l.
N. Zealand	200	or	50	or	250 g.	1.1 l.	and	4.5 l.
S. Africa	400	and	50	and	250 g.	1 l.	and	2 l.
U.K.	200	or	50	or	250 g.	1 l.	and	2 l.
U.S.A.	200	and	50	and	4)	1 l.	or	1 l.

1) within Europe from non-EEC countries
2) within Europe from EEC countries
3) countries outside Europe
4) a reasonable quantity

Currency restrictions. There are no restrictions on the import or export of money in any currency, but visitors importing the equivalent of L. 20,000,000 must fill out a customs form at the border upon entry.

DRIVING. To bring your car into Italy you will need:

● an international driving licence (non-Europeans)
● car registration papers
● Green Card (an extension to your regular insurance policy, making it valid specifically for Italy).
● national identity sticker for your car and the red warning triangle in case of breakdown.

D *Note:* Before leaving home, check with your automobile association about the latest regulations concerning *petrol coupons* (that give tourists access to cheaper fuel) in Italy, as they are constantly changing.

Driving conditions. Drive on the right. Pass on the left. Traffic on major roads has the right of way over traffic entering from side roads, but this, like all other traffic regulations, is frequently ignored, so beware. At intersections of roads of similar importance, the car on the right theoretically has the right of way. When passing other vehicles, or remaining in the left-hand (passing) lane, keep your directional indicator flashing. The use of seat belts became obligatory in 1989.

The motorways *(autostrada)* and most major national highways are of excellent quality, skilfully designed for fast driving. Florence is a major staging post on the famed Autostrada del Sole which runs the length of Italy, ensuring fast connections with Bologna, Milan, Rome and Naples. Each section of an *autostrada* requires payment of a toll: you collect a card from an automatic machine and pay at the other end for the distance travelled. Try to stock up on coins, since the toll booth attendants don't like making change. Every 2 kilometres on the *autostrada* there's an emergency call box marked SOS. There's often a lane to the extreme right for very slow traffic.

On country roads and even many main highways, you'll encounter bicycles, motorscooters, three-wheeled vehicles, and horse-drawn carts. Very often, such slow-moving vehicles have *no* lights, an obvious danger from dusk to dawn.

Last but not least: cars, buses, lorries (trucks) make use, indiscriminately, of their horns—in fact, blowing one's horn is an Italian attitude —so don't get flustered if it's done at you, and do it wherever it could help to warn of your impending arrival.

Fuel and oil. Fuel, sold at government-set price levels, comes as super (98–100 octane), lead free (95 octane) and normal (86–88 octane). Lead-free petrol is now common. Look for the pumps with green labels marked "Senza piombo" (without lead) or the abbreviation, SP. Diesel is also usually available. Oil comes in at least three varieties.

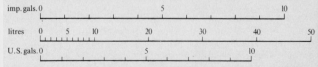

Speed limits. Speed limits in Italy are based on the car engine size. The speed limit on motorways is 130 kph for cars with engines more powerful than 1,000 cubic centimetres. Less powerful cars cannot exceed 110 kph. On other roads the limit is 90 kph. These maximum speeds may be revised again. Ask at your automobile association before departure.

The limit in built-up areas is usually 50 kph.

Driving in Florence. The centre of Florence (within the circle of avenues that surround it on both sides of the river Arno) has become ZTL (*Zona traffico limitato*—limited traffic zone). This applies from 7.30 a.m. to 6.30 p.m. Monday to Saturday, and only residents who have a special permit on their windscreens have access. Traffic police are usually stationed at the major entryways to stop anyone without a permit. You are allowed to enter only to reach a hotel. Ask a policeman for directions, as there have been many changes in the one-way system.

Look out, especially at intersections. Treat traffic lights which are theoretically in your favour with caution—don't take your priorities for granted.

Parking *(posteggio, parcheggio)*. Even if you can enter the historic centre after 6.30 p.m. and on Sundays, it is virtually impossible to park unless you can find space in a car park. There are numerous supervised car parks. Parking in the street is reserved for residents. Apart from the city centre parking places, some are available at Porta Romana (left bank), the Cascine (Piazza Vittorio Veneto) and Fortezza da Basso (Viale Filippo Strozzi). A smaller—but handy—parking facility is located in Piazza Libertà.

If you park your car overnight in the centre of Florence, be careful to heed the parking time allowance. Parking fines are now very heavy and the city is equipped with car-removal trucks that carry illegally parked cars to the Parco Macchine Requisite in Via Circondaria, 19. If this should happen, call (or ask your hotel to call) 35 52 31 to locate your car. Then you have to go there and pay to get it back.

Traffic police *(polizia stradale):* When they're in evidence, which is rather infrequently, Italian traffic police use motorcycles or Alfa-Romeos. All cities and many towns and villages have signs posted at the outskirts indicating the telephone number of the local traffic police headquarters or *Carabinieri*. In recent years police have become stricter about speeding, an Italian national pastime. They also frown on the widespread practice of "jumping the light". Fines are often paid on the spot. Ask for a receipt.

D   In cases of accidents on the road, call 112 for the *Carabinieri*. If your car is stolen or something is stolen from it, contact the Police Headquarters *(Questura)* in Florence at Via Zara, 2, and get them to draw up a certificate for the insurance.

Breakdowns: In Italy garages abound. Though most dislike dealing with any other make than Fiat, all major towns do have agencies for other models.

Dial 116 for breakdown service from the Automobile Club d'Italia.

Distance:

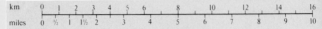

Road signs: Most road signs employed in Italy are international. But there are some written signs you might come across, too:

Accendere le luci	Use headlights
Curva pericolosa	Dangerous bend (curve)
Deviazione	Diversion (Detour)
Discesa pericolosa	Steep hill (with gradient percentage)
Divieto di sorpasso	No overtaking (passing)
Divieto di sosta	No stopping
Lavori in corso	Road works (Men working)
Parcheggio autorizzato	Parking allowed
Passaggio a livello	Level railway crossing
Passaggio limitato in altezza	Height restriction
Passaggio vietato ai pedoni	No pedestrians
Pericolo	Danger
Rallentare	Slow down
Senso vietato/unico	No entry/One-way street
Vietato l'ingresso	No entry
Zona pedonale	Pedestrian zone
ZTL	Limited traffic zone

(International) Driving Licence	**patente (internazionale)**
car registration papers	**libretto di circolazione**
Green Card	**carta verde**
Can I park here?	**Posso parcheggiare qui?**
Are we on the right road for ...?	**Siamo sulla strada giusta per ...?**
Fill the tank please ...	**Per favore, faccia il pieno de ...**
super/normal	**super/normale**
lead-free/diesel	**senza piombo/gasolio**

112

Check the oil/tires/battery.	**Controlli l'olio/i pneumatici/ la batteria.**
I've had a breakdown.	**Ho avuto un guasto.**
There's been an accident.	**C'è stato un incidente.**

DRUGS. Anyone possessing or selling drugs in Italy faces an unusually aroused police force and extremely severe legal penalties. No distinction is made between soft and hard drugs. Present maximum sentence is about eight years in prison and/or extremely stiff fines.

In every sense, drugs are a huge risk in Italy. Because of the monumental backlog in the nation's court cases, a person arrested on suspicion of a narcotics crime may spend as long as one year in jail before even being formally charged. Foreign consulates and embassies advise their citizens that there is no way for them to speed up the legal process.

ELECTRIC CURRENT (corrente elettrica). Florence now has 220-volt electric current. Non-Italian appliances may require a special plug to fit the sockets.

| I'd like an adaptor/a battery. | **Vorrei una presa complementare/ una batteria.** |

EMERGENCIES. The Florence telephone service has several emergency numbers. The main ones are listed below. If you don't speak Italian, try to find a local resident to help you call, or direct your problems to the English-speaking operators of the telephone assistance service, 116 (see also TOURIST INFORMATION OFFICES).

All-purpose emergency police number	113
Carabinieri	112
Assistance on the road—A.C.I.	116
Fire	115
Emergency medical service, holidays, night	436 15 41
Ambulance, first-aid	21 22 22

Depending on the nature of the problem, see also separate entries such as CONSULATES, MEDICAL CARE, POLICE, etc.

Please, can you place an emergency call for me to the…?	**Per favore, può fare per me una telefonata d'emergenza…?**
police	**alla polizia**
fire brigade	**ai pompieri**
hospital	**all'ospedale**

G **GUIDES and INTERPRETERS** *(guida; interprete).* Most hotels can arrange for multilingual guides or interpreters for any occasion. If you prefer, you can contact the Associazione Guide Turistiche:

Cooperativo Giotto, Viale Gramsci, 9a; tel. 247 81 88

We'd like an English-speaking guide.	**Desideriamo una guida che parla inglese.**
I need an English interpreter.	**Ho bisogno di un interprete d'inglese.**

H **HAIRDRESSERS and BARBERS** *(parrucchiere; barbiere).* It's wise for women to telephone for an appointment, although there are many hairdressers in Florence. Prices range from *haute coiffure* rates to very reasonable. As in most countries, the owner of a salon should never be tipped. Give the shampooer, manicurist or stylist up to 15% of the bill's total. Many hairdressing salons have facilities for facial treatments, make-up or massage.

I'd like a shampoo and set.	**Vorrei shampo e messa in piega.**
I want a...	**Voglio...**
haircut	**il taglio**
shave	**la rasatura**
blow-dry (brushing)	**asciugatura al fono**
permanent wave	**la permanente**
colour rinse	**un cachet**
manicure	**la manicure**
Don't cut it too short.	**Non li tagli troppo corti.**
A little more off (here).	**Un po' di più (qui).**

HITCH-HIKING *(autostop).* Hitch-hiking is forbidden on motorways in Italy; there are prominent *No Hitch-hiking* signs at entrances to the *autostrade.* Nonetheless, every summer thousands of young people hitch rides all over the country.

Can you give me a lift to...?	**Può darmi un passaggio fino a...?**

L **LANGUAGE.** Most hotel receptionists and sales staff in the shops and boutiques between the Duomo and Ponte Vecchio speak some English, French or German. Market stall-holders can at least tell you their prices in English. For the rest, and that includes the *Vigili Urbani* or city police, Italian or sign language is essential. Don't shrink from having a go at the language—Italians appreciate an effort.

There are numerous possibilities for summer language courses for foreigners both in Florence and in Siena (where a pure Italian is spoken). The Italian State Tourist Office in your country will supply information.

The Berlitz phrase book ITALIAN FOR TRAVELLERS covers most situations you are likely to encounter in Italy; also useful is the Italian-English/English-Italian pocket dictionary, containing a special menu-reader supplement.

Do you speak English?	**Parla inglese?**
I don't speak Italian.	**Non parlo italiano.**

LAUNDRY and DRY-CLEANING *(lavanderia; tintoria)*. Laundromats and dry-cleaners in the town are worth seeking out because hotels charge extremely high prices for such services. The yellow pages list addresses of establishments under "Lavanderia" and "Tintoria", or your hotel receptionist will tell you where the nearest facilities are to be found. The prices at a launderette are the same whether you do the job yourself or leave it with an attendant.

When will it be ready?	**Quando sarà pronto?**
I must have this for tomorrow morning.	**Mi serve per domani mattina.**

LOST PROPERTY *(oggetti smarriti)*. If you've mislaid or lost something away from your hotel, have the receptionist call the Ufficio Oggetti Smarriti, or go yourself to the general lost property office at

Via Circondaria, 19

For property lost on trains: Piazza dell'Unità, 1

Taxi and bus drivers often turn in lost articles to their headquarters.

Lost children. If you lose a child in Florence, don't worry. Italians everywhere adore children, and someone will unfailingly look after your youngster on the way to the nearest police station. Just contact the police at 3 69 11 immediately.

I've lost my passport/wallet/handbag.	**Ho perso il passaporto/portafoglio/la borsetta.**

MAPS. News-stands and tourist offices have a large selection of maps. You can obtain excellent free maps of the city and surrounding area from the tourist offices. The maps in this book were prepared by Falk-Verlag, Hamburg, who also publishes a complete map of Florence.

a street plan of...	**un piantina di ...**
a road map of this region	**una carta stradale di questa regione**

MEDICAL CARE. Citizens of Common Market countries are entitled to reimbursement for medical treatment in Italy, but ask your travel agent for details. Visitors whose insurance does not cover medical bills in Italy can take out a short-term holiday insurance policy before leaving home.

Pharmacies. Most chemists' shops *(farmacia)* are open during shopping hours, but some in Florence and its immediate vicinity are open all night. There's one in the main hall at Santa Maria Novella railway station. On weekends or public holidays the addresses of chemists on duty are published in the newspaper *La Nazione* and are also posted on every *farmacia* door. See also EMERGENCIES.

I need a doctor/a dentist.	**Ho bisogno di un medico/ dentista.**
I've a pain here.	**Ho un dolore qui.**
a stomach ache	**il mal di stomaco**
a fever	**la febbre**
a sunburn/sunstroke	**una scottatura di sole/un colpo di sole**

MEETING PEOPLE. Inordinately proud of their city, Florentines are only too pleased to show it off to visitors. Female tourists, however, may find they receive too much attention from the male population. Once beyond the usual opening line of "You speak English?" the offers are apt to include a personally conducted tour of Florence, special bargains in leatherware or taking the tourist's picture next to Michelangelo's *David*. If you're not interested, take no notice. Though Italian girls tend to go about in groups of two or three, they are by no means shy and retiring and are often pleased to practise their English.

In the *passeggiata,* or evening walk, Florentines of all ages stroll up and down discussing the day's news. The venue is usually a street in the centre of town, and the hour varies according to the season.

MONEY MATTERS

Currency. Italy's monetary unit is the *lira* (plural *lire,* abbreviated *L.* or *Lit.*).
  Coins: L. 5, 10, 20, 50, 100, 200 and 500.
  Banknotes: L. 1,000, 2,000, 5,000, 10,000, 50,000 and 100,000.
  For currency restrictions, see p.109.

Banking hours are from 8.20 a.m. to 1.20 p.m., Monday to Friday.

Currency exchange offices *(cambio).* Some exchange offices open on Saturday mornings. On Sundays and holidays, the exchange window at the Santa Maria Novella station is always open. Shop around to find the best rate for your cash since banks and exchange offices vary.

Credit cards and traveller's cheques. Most major hotels and many restaurants and shops now accept credit cards, but these do not entitle you to any special discounts. Traveller's cheques are welcome almost anywhere, with certain shops advertising a discount (perhaps 10%) on purchases by cheque. However, this advantage may be offset by a poor exchange rate. Paying a hotel bill in foreign currency or by traveller's cheque is not wise, since the hotel's exchange rate is usually lower than that of a *cambio.* Eurocheques are easily cashed in Italy.

Prices *(prezzo).* Florence still remains relatively inexpensive for British or North American visitors. The exception is the fashionable centre (Via de' Tornabuoni, Via de' Calzaiuoli) where prices compete with those of New York, Paris or Zurich. In bars or cafés, sitting down and having a waiter bring your *espresso* may cost you five times as much as having it at the counter. Cinemas and horse-drawn carriages are expensive, concerts and taxis reasonable, discotheques and nightclubs often ruinous.

I want to change some pounds/dollars.	**Desidero cambiare delle sterline/dei dollari.**
Do you accept traveller's cheques?	**Accetta traveller's cheques?**
Can I pay with this credit card?	**Posso pagare con la carta di credito?**

MUSEUM HOURS

Casa Buonarroti. 9.30 a.m.–6 p.m., Monday to Sunday, closed on Tuesdays.

M **Firenze com'era.** 9 a.m.–2 p.m., Monday to Wednesday and Friday to Saturday, 8 a.m.–1 p.m. on Sundays and holidays, closed on Thursdays.

Galleria dell'Academia. 9 a.m.–2 p.m., Tuesday to Saturday, till 1 p.m. on Sundays and holidays, closed on Mondays.

Galleria degli Uffizi. 9 a.m.–7 p.m., Tuesday to Saturday, till 1 p.m. on Sundays and holidays, closed on Mondays.

Museo della Fondazione Horne. 9 a.m.–1 p.m., Monday to Saturday, closed on Sundays and public holidays.

Museo Nazionale (Bargello). 9 a.m.–2 p.m., Tuesday to Saturday, 9 a.m.–1 p.m. Sundays and holidays. Closed on Mondays.

Museo dell'Opera di Santa Maria del Fiore. 9 a.m.–7.30 p.m. in summer, 9 a.m.–6 p.m. in winter. Closed on public holidays.

Museo di San Marco. 9 a.m.–2 p.m., Tuesday to Saturday, till 1 p.m. on Sundays and holidays, closed on Mondays.

Palazzo Pitti. 9 a.m.–2 p.m., Tuesday to Saturday, till 1 p.m. on Sundays and holidays, closed on Mondays.

Palazzo Vecchio (Palazzo della Signoria). 9 a.m.–7 p.m., Monday to Friday, 8 a.m.–1 p.m. on Sundays and holidays, closed on Saturdays.

N **NEWSPAPERS and MAGAZINES** *(giornale; rivista).* Many major British and continental newspapers and magazines are on sale at kiosks—usually a day late—in the centre of Florence, at some hotels and at the station. But English-language periodicals are expensive. The Paris-based *International Herald Tribune,* which does arrive the same day, carries news and full U.S. stock-market quotations. Florence's most widely read daily, *La Nazione,* carries information on events, entertainment and cinemas and even devotes a column to activities for Florence's summer tourists.

P **PHOTOGRAPHY.** Central Florence can pose some problems to would-be photographers—there's seldom enough clear distance in which to photograph a church or a monument without cutting part of it out. But don't be discouraged, you can still bring off some first-class shots with a pocket camera. In summer, Florence's early morning or late afternoon sun is best for panoramic views (from the Piazzale Michelangelo).

Photography is allowed in all state-owned museums provided you use neither flash nor tripod. In municipal museums you need special permission.

All major brands and sizes of film are obtainable in Florence, but prices are higher than in most other countries.

I'd like a film for this camera.	**Vorrei una pellicola per questa macchina fotografica.**
a colour-slide film	**una pellicola di diapositive**
a film for colour prints	**una pellicola per fotografie a colori**
35-mm film	**una pellicola trentacinque millimetri**
How long will it take to develop this film?	**Quanto tempo ci vuole per sviluppare questa pellicola?**
May I take a picture?	**Posso fare una fotografia?**

POLICE. Florence's city police, *Vigili Urbani,* handle traffic, hand out parking fines and perform other routine police tasks. While rarely speaking a foreign language, *Vigili Urbani* are courteous and helpful to tourists.

The *Carabinieri,* a paramilitary force, wear light brown or blue uniforms and peaked caps, and deal with violent or serious crimes and demonstrations.

Outside of towns, the *Polizia Stradale* patrol the highways and byways (see under DRIVING).

Some police telephone numbers:

Vigili Urbani H.Q. *(Questura)*	4 97 71
Carabinieri, for emergencies	112
Polizia Stradale	57 77 77
Stolen vehicles department	3 69 11

There's also the all-purpose emergency number, 113, which will get you police assistance.

Where's the nearest police station?	**Dov'è il più vicino posto di polizia?**

PUBLIC HOLIDAYS *(festa).* Banks, government institutions, most shops and some museums are closed on all national holidays, as well

P as at least half a day for the Florentines' special holiday on the 24th of June. This is the day commemorating the town's patron saint, Giovanni Battista (John the Baptist). The week or ten days around August 15 *(Ferragosto)* sees almost everything in Florence closed except hotels, a few shops, chemists', cafés and restaurants and some of the major sightseeing attractions.

January 1	*Capodanno* or *Primo dell'Anno*	New Year's Day
January 6	*Epifania*	Epiphany
April 25	*Festa della Liberazione*	Liberation Day
May 1	*Festa del Lavoro*	Labour Day
August 15	*Ferragosto*	Assumption Day
November 1	*Ognissanti*	All Saints' Day
December 8	*Immacolata Concezione*	Immaculate Conception
December 25	*Natale*	Christmas Day
December 26	*Santo Stefano*	Saint Stephen's Day
Movable date:	*Lunedì di Pasqua*	Easter Monday

Are you open tomorrow? **È aperto domani?**

R **RADIO and TV** *(radio; televisione)*. The Italian state radio and TV network is the RAI. During the tourist season, RAI radio broadcasts news in English from Monday to Saturday at 10 a.m. and on Sundays at 9.30 a.m. predominantly about Italian affairs. Vatican Radio carries foreign-language religious news programmes at various times during the day. Shortwave radio reception in Florence is excellent throughout the night and part of the day. British (BBC), American (VOA) and Canadian (CBC) programmes are easily obtained on modest transistor radios. The American Southern European Broadcast (SEB) from Vicenza can be heard on regular AM radio (middle or medium wave). TV Montecarlo broadcasts Dan Rathers' American evening news report the following morning at 7.30 a.m. and repeats it at 8 a.m. from Tuesday to Saturday.

RELIGIOUS SERVICES *(funzione religiosa, messa)*. The Duomo (Sat. at 5 p.m.) and a few other churches celebrate mass in English. **120** Confession can be made in English in most churches in the centre.

English-language services for non-Catholic denominations:

American Episcopalian: St. James', Via B. Rucellai, 9

Anglican: St. Mark's, Via Maggio, 16

Christian Science: Via della Spada, 1

Jewish: synagogue at Via Farini, 4

SIESTA. For the noon break in the winter, most shops and stores close from 1 p.m. to 3.30 p.m. In the summer (June–September), this becomes 1 to 4 p.m., and they stay open fill 8 p.m. In the centre, many shops do not close at lunchtime during the tourist season (Easter to September). Many large department stores and supermarkets now are open throughout the lunch break, all year round.

TIME DIFFERENCES. Italy follows Central European Time (GMT +1), and from April to September clocks are put one hour ahead (= GMT+ 2). Summer time chart:

New York	London	Italy	Jo'burg	Sydney	Auckland
6 a.m.	11 a.m.	noon	noon	8 p.m.	10 p.m.

What time is it?   **Che ore sono?**

TIPPING. Though a service charge is added to most restaurant bills, it is customary to leave an additional tip. It is also in order to hand the bellboys, doormen, hat check attendants, garage attendants, etc., a coin or two for their service.

The chart below gives some suggestions as to what to leave.

Hotel porter, per bag	L. 1,000
Maid, per day	L. 1,000–2,000
Lavatory attendant	L. 300
Waiter	10%
Taxi driver	10%
Haidresser/barber	up to 15%
Tour guide	10%

T **TOILETS.** You'll find public toilets in most museums and galleries; restaurants, bars, cafés and large stores usually have facilities; airports and train stations always do. They may be designated in different ways: W.C. (for water closet) with the picture of a man or woman; sometimes the wording will be in Italian—*Uomini* (men) or *Donne* (women). The most confusing label for foreigners is *Signori* (men—with a final *i*) and *Signore* (women—with a final *e*).

Where are the toilets?   **Dove sono i gabinetti?**

TOURIST INFORMATION OFFICES. Italian State Tourist Offices (in America called Italian Government Travel Offices) are maintained in many countries throughout the world. Their Italian name: Ente Nazionale Italiano per il Turismo, abbreviated E.N.I.T.

Australia and New Zealand. c/o Italian Government Tourist Office, Lion's Building, 1-1-2 Moto Akasaka, Minatu-Ku, Tokyo 107; tel. (3) 478-2051

Canada. 1, Place Ville-Marie, Suite 1914, Montreal H3B 3M9, Que.; tel. (514) 849-8351

Eire. 47, Merrion Square, Dublin 2; tel. (3531) 766-397

South Africa. E.N.I.T., P.O. Box 6507, Johannesburg 2000

United Kingdom. 1, Princes Street, London W1 8AY; tel. (071) 408-1254

U.S.A. 500 N. Michigan Avenue, Chicago, IL 60611; tel. (312) 644-0990
630 Fifth Avenue, New York, NY 10020; tel. (212) 245 4822/23/24
360 Post Street, Suite 801, San Francisco, CA 94108; tel. (415) 392-5266

In **Florence,** refer to the tourist information office at:
Via Cavour I/R, 50129 Firenze; tel. 27 60 382

If you're interested in visiting local farms and Chianti vineyards, contact Agriturist, at:
Piazza S. Firenze, 3; tel. 28 78 38

Telephone assistance service:
The English-speaking operators here will answer your questions and give advice. They also serve as trouble shooters, offering help to visitors who have problems. Dial 116 anywhere in Italy.

122 Where's the tourist office?   **Dov'è l'ufficio turistico?**

Buses *(autobus)*. Florence has about 40 main city and suburban bus routes. For all information about buses, and for a useful free bus map, go to the A.T.A.F. office at Piazza del Duomo, 57r.

You must buy your bus ticket in advance at a tobacconist or bar. When you board a bus—either at the front door beside the bus driver or at the back door (centre door is for exit only), punch your ticket in the *red* machine. Long-distance bus companies cover the whole of Tuscany, and go as far as Venice and Rome. Your hotel or any travel agent will supply information.

Taxis *(taxi)*. Florence's taxis may be picked up at a taxi rank or, more usually, obtained by telephone (4798 and 4390). Cabs are yellow. Fares are indicated on meters, plus extra charges for luggage, station pick-ups and for night rides. A 10% tip is in order, or more if the driver has been especially helpful.

Trains *(treno)*. If you haven't booked, it is wise to arrive at the station at least 20 minutes before departure to be sure of a seat: Italy's trains are often very crowded. The following list describes the various types of trains:

Eurocity (EC)	International express; first and second class; surcharge on many.
Intercity (IC)/ Rapido	High-speed super-express, first class only (ticket includes seat reservation, newspaper refreshments). Also first and second class; stops at main stations; surcharge.
Espresso (Expr.)	Long-distance train, stopping at main stations.
Diretto (Dir.)	Slower than the *Espresso,* it makes a number of local stops.
Locale (L)	Local train which stops at almost every station.
Metropolitana (servizi dedicati)	Connecting service from airports and sea ports to major cities.

T

Littorina	Small diesel train used on short runs.		
Carozza ristorante	*Vagone letto*	*Carozza cuccette*	*Bagagliaio*
Dining car	Sleeping car with individual compartments and washing facilities	Sleeping berth car (couchette); blankets and pillows	Guard's van (baggage car); normally only registered luggage permitted

When's the next bus/train to…?	**Quando parte il prossimo autobus/treno per…?**
I want a ticket to…	**Vorrei un biglietto per…**
single (one-way)	**andata**
return (round-trip)	**andata e ritorno**
first/second class	**prima/seconda classe**
Will you tell me when to get off?	**Può dirmi quando devo scendere?**
Where can I get a taxi?	**Dove posso trovare un taxi?**
What's the fare to…?	**Qual è la tariffa per…?**

W **WATER** *(acqua)*. Florence's tap-water is not very tasty, but it's drinkable. One of the only places where water still actually tastes natural is in the inner courtyard of the Palazzo Pitti. You'll see local people filling bottles and other containers at its two fountains.

With meals, take wine and/or bottled mineral water. Mineral waters are popularly believed to help not only digestion, but an incredible array of afflictions, and there's certainly something to it. There'll be a sign reading *acqua non potabile* where water is not for drinking.

a bottle of mineral water carbonated/non-carbonated	**una bottiglia di acqua minerale gasata/naturale**

SOME USEFUL EXPRESSIONS

yes/no	**sì/no**
please/thank you	**per favore/grazie**
excuse me/you're welcome	**mi scusi/prego**
where/when/how	**dove/quando/come**
how long/how far	**quanto tempo/quanto dista**
yesterday/today/tomorrow	**ieri/oggi/domani**
day/week/month/year	**giorno/settimana/mese/anno**
left/right	**sinistra/destra**
up/down	**su/giù**
good/bad	**buono/cattivo**
big/small	**grande/piccolo**
cheap/expensive	**buon mercato/caro**
hot/cold	**caldo/freddo**
old/new	**vecchio/nuovo**
open/closed	**aperto/chiuso**
free (vacant)/occupied	**libero/occupato**
near/far	**vicino/lontano**
early/late	**presto/tardi**
quick/slow	**rapido/lento**
full/empty	**pieno/vuoto**
easy/difficult	**facile/difficile**
right/wrong	**giusto/sbagliato**
here/there	**qui/là**
Does anyone here speak English?	**C'è qualcuno qui che parla inglese?**
I don't understand.	**Non capisco.**
Please write it down.	**Lo scriva, per favore.**
Waiter/Waitress, please.	**Cameriere!/Cameriera!** (or **Senta!** = "listen")
I'd like...	**Vorrei...**
How much is that?	**Quant'è?**
Have you something less expensive?	**Ha qualcosa di meno caro?**
What time is it?	**Che ore sono?**
Just a minute.	**Un attimo.**
Help me, please.	**Per favore, mi aiuti.**

Index

An asterisk (*) next to a page number indicates a map reference.